AN ALBAN INSTITUTE
PUBLICATION

THE ONCE AND FUTURE CHURCH

REINVENTING THE CONGREGATION FOR A NEW MISSION FRONTIER

BY LOREN B. MEAD

Library of Congress Catalog Card Number 91-72968
ISBN 1-56699-050-5

CONTENTS

INTRODUCTION

God is always calling us to be more than we have been.

In this book I will try to spell out some of the implications of that statement for the world I know best—the Churches. My reasons are very simple: It is my conviction that religious congregations are the most important carriers of meaning that we have, with one exception. They are the most important ground of purpose and direction that we have, with one exception. They are the most important source of an essential element of life—human community—with one exception.

The one exception is the human family. The reason the family is not the subject of this book is that it is not my area of expertise or calling. My thing—the thing I have been called to think about, struggle with, work on—is the religious congregation. For six decades now, I have inhabited them, enjoyed them, been frustrated by them, earned a living from them, and tried to understand them.

And, although I assume the primacy of the human family in all the ways noted above, I am also bold enough to note that even families—in my experience—run into trouble if they lose their connection to a religion- and value-bearing community—the kind of community I have experienced only in a congregation.

I come to this task from a very limited view; as a Christian and an Episcopalian, almost classically "mainline Protestant," I see what is going on through those lenses. I see more than that and my experience is much broader, but those are my lenses and they influence how I see whatever I see. I also have other lenses that limit me in one sense and give me perspective in another—male, American, white, southern, born during the Depression. In all these ways I bring perceptions and perspec-

tives that help me see some things as no one else can, but that make me
blind to other things. I have learned how to overcome some areas of
blindness, but I remain sensitive to the limits of my vision.

Yet I am bold enough to say that even from a limited perspective
what I have to say speaks of larger realities and a larger call, one much
more universal than my experience, my perspective, or my vision. What
I see of God's call in my portion of the vineyard is consistent, I believe,
with the call of God in other parts of the vineyard and in other institutions in which we live and move. I do not think that God is calling just
the Church or just religious congregations—God's call is for all of creation. And some of the groaning and travailing results from our having to
deal with God's unsettling call in all of our institutions.

In this book I want to spell out the call that I perceive to be troubling
the waters today. For I do see the turmoil and uncertainty, the civil wars
and professional burnouts of religious institutions today as evidence of
the troubled waters that always indicate the potential presence of God's
healing powers. So long as we see those disturbing institutional issues
simply as problems to be solved, we may miss out on the call that lies
within them.

In the beginning I will talk about how mission has always shaped
the life of the Church. I will try to point out the change in our way of
thinking about mission that confuses much of what we are now doing. I
will point to pressure points in the lives of congregations and religious
institutions that shape the evolution of those structures toward new
forms; I will describe the large shifts in religious consciousness we are
experiencing; and I will point to dimensions of these changes that touch
other institutions. Finally I want to spell out what I think the call is and
what implications it has for the institutional structures we must invent to
carry us into the next century.

God is always calling us to be more than what we have been.

Never has that been more true than it is today. Never has it been
more true for anyone than it is today for those of us who are related to
religious congregations. Never before have those in religious congregations had more—potentially—to give to the other structures of society.

In putting forth these ideas I want to acknowledge my indebtedness
to those with whom I have worked these past four decades: lay persons,
clergy, teachers of many denominations. I note especially my colleagues
at The Alban Institute.

Celia Hahn has given the kind of support and encouragement that kept me on track when I wanted to quit. Mary Forbes performed miracles in deciphering my notes and locating things I lost on my computer disks.

Four others gave me specific feedback and criticism—Bob Isaksen, Lutheran bishop of the New England Synod (ELCA); Susan Heath, Canon Theologian of Trinity Cathedral, Columbia, South Carolina; Carl Dudley of McCormick Theological Seminary and The Center for Church and Community in Chicago; and Bill Craddock, lay theologian. Bruce Boston gave immense help in shaping the final manuscript. If anything is wrong with this book, as far as I am concerned, I am sure it's *their* fault!

CHAPTER I

The Challenge of the Congregation

Across the face of the country, no feature is more pronounced than the presence of places of worship wherever people live.

Small southern towns with only two roads crossing will have four fortress-like parish churches facing across the intersection. From a hilltop anywhere in New England, one can locate villages by the white spires of local churches poking up through the green foliage. Major urban centers house enormous buildings perched on corners, far more impressive than the few people who straggle through decaying streets to attend worship there. Ethnic neighborhoods boast houses of worship where English is rarely or never spoken by the older generation. Some ghettoes are home for great worshipping congregations whose membership is drawn from all over a metropolitan center.

Churches are found in the open country with no houses in sight, serving far-flung farm families. Others are behind urban storefronts serving very small communities in cities of millions.

A number, many in the Sunbelt, are major, fast-growing enterprises of publishing, worship, and service, dealing with congregations as large as small towns, led by corporate planning, and enjoying executive leadership of the most sophisticated kind. Some are called "megachurches" that carry on ministries through sophisticated media facilities and through hundreds of small groups.

Some are closed in upon themselves, while others eagerly engage the community and even the world with outreach or mission activities. Some are refuges of a narrow elitism; others work hard at breaking down barriers to become inclusive.

Some of them struggle from week to week just to survive, while others manage assets in the tens of millions. Some have no professional, paid staff, while others have rank on rank of professional and volunteer people-power. Some struggle to meet weekly, others have as much activity as a shopping mall seven days a week. Some are one-of-a-kind, accountable only to themselves; others are closely linked in regional and national networks.

Each one tends to be very important to many of its members. Each one also has within it members who are critical of it and who want it to be "more" or "better" than it is.

Over the centuries since 1607, congregations have been a special part of the social glue that de Toqueville described as characteristic of this nation. They have been a center of community life. They have been an anchor, a place of stability, holding up a transcendent vision of the meaning of life as a new nation struggled to understand and build a society. Congregations have grounded the nation in the biblical story that gave words and ideas to America's great moments—from the time of the Pilgrims to July 4, 1776, from Gettysburg to the Birmingham jail. Congregations contributed not only to the framing of statements but to people's ability to hear the messages of those critical times.

Congregations have also been places of refuge and identity for those from distant lands who spoke different languages, making possible the first steps of the immigrant into a new nation.

Less dramatically, but perhaps even more importantly, congregations have also been a place for retreat and regrouping in the face of hurt, distress, or injustice. They have healed and restored the spirits of those broken by deliberate cruelty and by simple human tragedy. To this day it is to congregations that people—even many who find formal beliefs and doctrines foreign to their style of life—come to face death, loss, birth, the discovery of love, the collapse of hope.

This book is about that institution, the congregation, because the congregation is at a critical point of change.

During the years in which refugees and pioneers came to America from Europe, then from other lands, congregational forms were imported, primarily from western and northern Europe. Churches of Reformation heritage—Anglican, Presbyterian, Congregational—became established in some colonies by law, in others by custom. When the founders of the nation, 200 years later, chose to reject the idea of a legally established church, they did so in a society in which the informal coalition of those three traditions made for a de facto establishment that still influences us today. That establishment expanded and changed many times as new partners first challenged, then were absorbed into it: Methodists, Lutherans, Catholics. Will Herberg, writing in the late 1950s, described the new establishment in the title of his book as *Protestant, Catholic, Jew.* Since he wrote, evangelicals and African-American Protestants have stretched the meaning of the establishment once again, and each component has become more diverse. At the same time, the earlier partners in the coalition have undergone change and diversification. The Episcopalians, the Presbyterians, and the Congregationalists of the late 20th century are distant cousins of those who sat in the Continental Congress and formed a nation.

Local churches were born into this culture of establishment, whether they approved of it and joined it, or disapproved and tried to remain apart from it. Denominations—those peculiarly American inventions— became families of identity for congregations within the larger community of the informal establishment.

The most articulate and self-assured of the partners in this establishment were those who came to it earliest, those identified as "the mainline" churches. The longer they had been accepted as partners in the establishment, the more mainline they tended to be. Evangelical and fundamentalist latecomers, although uncomfortable with the role, became more and more visible, establishment, and mainline as the original partners diminished in size and influence after the 1950s.

The much documented collapse of mainline religion was most visible as a collapse of denominational structures and agencies that themselves were born mostly in this century. The structure of agencies, boards, and commissions invented by the American religious denominations in the first half of the 20th century was the last flowering of a great and creative age when the churches were powered by a strong, clear, uniform paradigm of mission. The rich variety of national and regional church structures developed by 1960 were supported because thousands of local congregations knew in their bones that that was the way to support the mission that had been laid upon the church. The members of local congregations had a clear sense of what that mission was, and they supported it with some enthusiasm.

American denominations came out of World War II with a heady sense of how victory is won and with an unlimited enthusiasm for getting on with mission. Many of the denominations built their own Pentagons and formed a grand alliance to achieve mission goals. They expanded their training camps by enlarging their seminaries. Members were generous in providing capital funds and buildings. New congregations sprouted on the suburban frontier. Nowhere was there a more visible symbol of the consensus of the mission crusade than in the Interchurch Center, the so-called "God-Box" at 475 Riverside Drive in New York.

The dream of the new alliance for ministry and mission was never fulfilled. The National Council of Churches, a symbol of the great alliance, is today a shadow of what it was. The halls of the God-Box no longer bustle as once they did. New, separate Pentagons have sprouted in Chicago, Louisville, and Cleveland as old allies struggle for vision, clarity, and direction.

Historians, sociologists, anthropologists, and theologians are struggling right now to try to understand what happened. We may never know all of it. I try to describe in Chapter Two some of what I understand happened.

The result, however, was that in congregation after congregation, person after person, agency after agency, the one clear paradigm of mission stopped being clear. In one denomination after another, the consensus disappeared. Voices became discordant. Mission, which had once been both central rallying cry and basic assumption, became instead a subject of debate and disagreement. What had been clear simply was not clear any more. Instead of having a shared sense of one crusade in which all were engaged and to which all were committed, we began to be aware of different agendas, conflicting demands, and needs for ministry.

Perhaps the next steps were inevitable. People and congregations who were prepared to make sacrifices to support a mission consensus found it hard to generate enthusiasm and conviction for a more complicated reality. One need only look at the national capacity to make sacrifices for what seemed a clear crusade in World War II and the very different national response to the complex, confused, unclear tasks of the Vietnam conflict. In congregation after congregation, person after person, agency after agency, a consensus about mission ceased to have compelling power. The energy supporting the institutional infrastructure evaporated.

This book argues that three things are happening around us simultaneously:

First, our present confusion about mission hides the fact that we are facing a fundamental change in how we understand the mission of the church. Beneath the confusion we are being stretched between a great vision of the past and a new vision that is not yet fully formed.

Second, local congregations are now being challenged to move from a passive, responding role in support of mission to a front-line, active role. The familiar roles of laity, clergy, executive, bishop, church council, and denominational bureaucrat are in profound transition all around us.

Third, institutional structures and forms developed to support one vision of our mission are rapidly collapsing. I argue that we are being called to invent or reinvent structures and forms that will serve the new mission as well as the old structures served the old vision. I believe that we are being called to be midwives for a new church, working to help our present forms and structures give birth to forms appropriate for the new mission of the church.

I am not sanguine, as I look around the churches, about the institutional response to this time of challenge when support for the traditional structures and roles is evaporating. All too often I see pessimism, depression, and defeat in the lay leaders, clergy, and denominational leaders we depend on for the reinvention of the church.

In recent years I have seen three kinds of responses in denominational systems:

1) Frantic effort to recapture the initiative, to get "ahead of the curve" and to develop a NEW PROGRAM so compelling that it will reattract all the eroded support. I see regional and national leaders, particularly, making more and more aggressive promises, holding up grander visions, calling their flocks to larger hopes. In almost every case the result is that the clock is not turned back, the resources continue to decline—with an occasional hiccup of growth—and those leaders end up with larger tasks, promises, and commitments but even fewer resources and staff.

Restructuring, relocation of offices, realignment of staffs—behind these names we try to hide what is going on. It is like fibrillation, in which a heart under stress, pumping more and more rapidly, but without coordination, actually begins to work against itself, pumping less and less blood to the body.

2) Holding steady and hoping for the best—if not for divine intervention—is a second strategy some are trying. The Catholic Church's attitude toward the crisis of a shortfall in priestly vocations is one example. All those denominational studies of how losses of members or money have "bottomed out" are other examples.

Still other signs of desperation are the periodic infusions of capital (through major gift drives, "major mission funding" efforts, etc.) which try to shore up programs that are dying because people are no longer convinced that they serve a mission at all and no longer support worn out programs with enthusiasm.

My point is that all too often these responses represent a vain hope that somehow things will change. They are ways of shoring up parts of a system that has stopped working. They keep our attention and resources from efforts to build a more effective system.

3) A third strategy, the one I obviously prefer, requires moving ahead into a new paradigm of mission, rebuilding and reinventing the church as we go. This choice would be simple to make if two things were clear—what the new paradigm really *is*, and how we determine which parts of the collapsing system we need to keep to make it in the new era. In this book I assume that we have no viable alternative to this third option, even though most denominational responses so far have been along the lines of the first two.

We face a significant problem: Our need for a clear consensus on mission from which we can construct the forms of a new church is no guarantee that we can find it. There is no certainty that we shall be led to a sense of mission as compelling as the one that drove previous generations. That time of clarity may be over. The denominational families with which most of us have had a love-hate relationship for years may have already become antiquarian relics. God may have a more challenging future in store for us, calling us out of these structures altogether.

We must also be aware of our temptation to expend all our resources and energy in shoring up collapsing structures, holding onto the familiar long after it has lost its possibility for new life. One inelegant rule of thumb I use in this area is what I call the "M-T-M ratio." By that I try to state how long I think a particular organization deserves to have mouth-to-mouth resuscitation practiced on it. Everybody needs help from time to time, but I see all too many religious organizations that drew their last unassisted breath a decade ago.

Within all of this, the local congregation is critical. The congregation is where people touch the church and are touched by it. It is there that literally millions of people are struggling to understand their own personal sense of mission and to get the strength to pursue it. The congregation is where new people are brought into a faith-heritage that connects them to the biblical story and to the life of the people of God.

It is also there that urgency for mission is already being felt and articulated. It is there that the new structures and roles must be discovered to undergird that mission. Much of this book is about just that.

Our task now is to look at how our vision of the mission of the church came into sharp focus, shaping the way we organized ourselves and the roles we assigned each other to carry out that mission. After acknowledging what that vision produced, we need to look at how that clarity came to lose its sharp focus. Only then can we look at an emerging sense of mission and begin to forecast the kinds of changes that will require ordering our lives within the church.

CHAPTER II

Paradigms Lost

Twice before the most recent change in its idea of mission, the church has been challenged to reorder its understanding of self and world. In the very earliest days it struggled about whether it was identical to or different from its Jewish roots. Simultaneously, it was trying to be related to and distinguished from the Greco-Roman world in which it spread. Looking back with the perspective of history, we see a paradigm emerge —the paradigm of the apostolic age. Generations later, when the new faith became the official faith of the Roman Empire, a reorientation occurred throughout the institution. Like the first, that reorientation was the church's attempt to relate to its social environment and accomplish its mission. I call the consciousness that developed out of that time the paradigm of the age of Christendom.

In our own time, that second paradigm is breaking apart. Its successor, a third paradigm, has yet to appear fully.

With each change of paradigm, roles and relationships change and power shifts. New structures develop. New directions emerge. Things that were of great value in one age become useless in the next. Times of transition between ages and paradigms are times of confusion and tumult.

But always, the focus is mission. The confusion and tumult, the upsetting of roles, structures, and relationships has the same purpose: to readdress the question of mission in a new time.

During those times of change, the confusion of the outside world was reflected in turbulence within the church, especially in local parishes and congregations. After generations of turbulence and change, a new self-understanding emerged so that the roles, relationships, and tasks focused outward to serve a new sense of mission.

This intimate conversation between a human group and its environment is characteristic of all institutions. It is in that conversation that the group reassesses what it is and what it values. But the conversation also helps it define its relationship or mission to that world surrounding it.

For two millenia the church has struggled with its image of itself and its image of the world outside. The church experienced a special pressure emerging from its belief that its Lord had given it a double-edged commandment—it was to engage with the world, to love the world, to serve the world, to convert the world. And yet it was also to maintain itself as in some sense "distinct from" the world. It was to be a "peculiar people," as Peter put it, but the peculiarity had much to do with caring for and serving that world for God.

The history of the church and its mission has been the struggle to carry out the two sides of that commission. Both the church and the world are always in flux, but usually we bring to that constant change a stable and unchanging paradigm, a mind-set that sometimes lasts for centuries. Sooner or later, however, the thousands of minute shifts and changes bring such pressure to bear that the stable mind-set cracks, shifts, or falls apart. That has happened to us.

Twice before in our history, a broad enough consensus developed about who the church was and how it related, in mission, to the world, so that a single vision became dominant (although it was never uniformly held). Twice before the church has faced such a complete upsetting of the old paradigm that life was disrupted and structures were reordered to form a new one. In our time, it is happening again. The importance of what is happening now, however, is that while we have experienced the disintegration and disruption of the old, the new paradigm has not yet appeared.

The basic idea of this book is that when that new paradigm does appear, it will emerge from a new sense of the church's mission, giving it a new clarity and focus.

The Apostolic Paradigm

The first time of tumult was the first generations after Jesus. It resulted in the Apostolic Paradigm.

Jesus articulated a powerful call for a people to be sent (*apostellein*, to send forth) to serve and convert the world, to care for the sick, the prisoner and the widow, the fatherless and the poor. As far as we can tell from the literature of the first and second centuries, different styles and different structures emerged in different places to carry out those tasks. Collegial and monarchical structures coexisted side by side. Communal experiments held sway in some places. Different functions and roles emerged—apostle, teacher, healer, bishop, presbyter, deacon, and a dozen more. Some fought to retain close links with the Jewish community; others fought to distance themselves from that community.

The turbulence came from the community's search for its identity in mission. Because these people knew they had been called and commissioned by their Lord to carry on his loving service in the world, they had big, pressing questions. They were driven to ask "Who are we in relationship to those around us? To whom are we sent?" They struggled with their answers as they worshiped week by week and listened to the stories about Jesus and his mission. It was out of their life in their world as they worked on these questions and stories that the paradigm of the apostolic age emerged.

The early church was conscious of itself as a faithful people surrounded by an hostile environment to which each member was called to witness to God's love in Christ. They were called to be evangelists, in the biblical sense of the word—those who bear good news. Their task was to carry into a hostile world the good news of healing, love, and salvation.

The central reality of this church was a local community, a congregation "called out" (*ekklesia*) of the world. It was a community that lived by the power and the values of Jesus. That power and those values were preserved and shared within the intimate community through apostolic teaching and preaching, through fellowship itself, and through ritual acts, preeminently the sharing of the bread and wine of the Eucharist. You gained entrance into this community only when the community was convinced that you also held those values and had been born into that power. The community was intense and personal. Belonging to it was an experience of being in immediate touch with God's Spirit.

It was no Pollyanna community. The epistles of the New Testament describe people and groups that experienced fractures and conflict, anger and division, as well as peace and joy.

The other side of this community image was an image of a world environment that was hostile to what the church stood for. The world was not neutral, it was opposed to the community. Each group of Christians was an illicit community, proscribed by the laws of the land. In many places, it was a capital offense to consort with or be a Christian.

A community formed of common values and shaped by a story within a larger, hostile environment: that was part of the story of the Apostolic Paradigm.

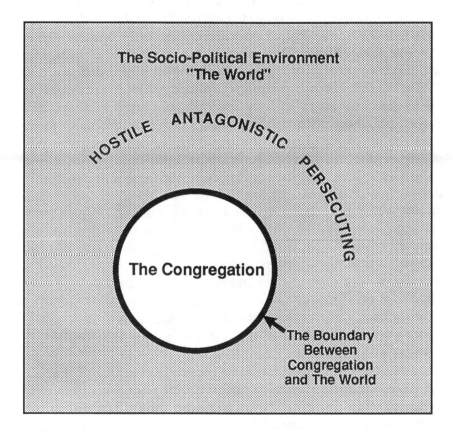

Figure 1

The other side of the paradigm, however, was the commission built into the story that formed the community. The community was called to reach out *to* the environment. The community was to "go into the world," to "be in the world but not of it." It could not be true to its nature and play it safe. Its marching orders were to engage the world, not withdraw from it. In spite of the world's aversion to what the church stood for, the church's people were required to engage with it, to witness to their Lord right in the middle of the hostile environment.

Put differently, the congregation came to see that its front door was the frontier into mission. They were impelled to take the life they shared within the congregation and, in its power, cross over the boundary into the hostile world outside. They called it "witnessing," the Greek word for which is "martyr." The irony of their being is in that word.

The life of the church as institution was shaped by this paradigm. There was a clear "inside" and "outside." So great was the difference between them that entry into the community from the world outside was a dramatic and powerful event. In baptism the person dramatized a symbolic death to the things of the world and a new birth into the way of the cross. The leaders led the community in teaching and preaching the story and in recreating the community in the act of thanksgiving (Eucharist) that symbolized salvation to a new life in a new world. The roles of the congregation fit the mission to the world—servant-ministers carried food to the hungry and healers cared for the sick. Gradually, as the need arose, regional leaders were appointed or emerged to help connect the communities. Traveling teachers and troubleshooters like Paul and Barnabas became prominent.

An intimate community, whose being demanded that it serve and care for a world hostile to itself: that is a fuller picture of the Apostolic Paradigm. *(See Figure 2.)*

Much of the congregation's life was defined by its sense of being on the mission frontier to a hostile world. But it also perceived that the meaning of its life was to build up its members with the courage, strength, and skill to communicate God's good news within that hostile world. Its internal task was to order its life, to establish roles and relationships that nurtured the members of the congregation in the mission that involved each member. Members perceived that the power to engage in that mission—the crossing of the missionary boundary—came from the Holy Spirit.

The church that emerged from the first three centuries had adopted structures and roles to do that kind of mission. The Apostolic Paradigm was the mind-set the church adopted to understand its mission.

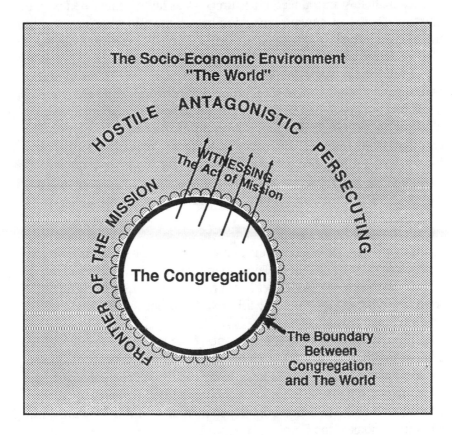

Figure 2

The Christendom Paradigm

Beginning in the fourth century a new paradigm began to emerge. Again, the emergence of the paradigm took time. This time the change took centuries, not just a few generations. I call it the Christendom Paradigm. It was begun by the conversion of the Emperor Constantine in

313 A.D. and grew progressively as Christianity became in name and law the official religion of the Empire.

The critical difference, once this paradigm settled in, was that by law the church was identified with the Empire. The world—the world that immediately surrounded the church—was legally identified with the church. There was now no separation between world and church within the Empire. The law removed the hostility from the environment but also made the environment and the church identical.

I want to say that again, in a slightly different way. Instead of the congregation being a small local group that constituted the church in that place, the understanding of the congregation had been enlarged to include everything in the Empire. The congregation was the church; the church was the Empire. There was no boundary between people on the local scene, defining one group as "church" and another as "world." The missionary frontier disappeared from the doorstep of the congregation and became, in effect, the political boundary of the society itself, far away.

Some implications of this change are obvious. No longer is the ordinary participant in a congregation personally and intimately on the mission frontier. The individual is no longer called to "witness" in a hostile environment. No longer is she or he supposed to be different from any other citizen. Indeed, citizenship has become identical with one's religious responsibility.

The other side is equally important. The missionary frontier on the edge of the Empire now becomes the responsibility of the professional —the soldier's job for the political realm and the specially designated missionary's job for the religious realm. In addition, however, the missionary understands that winning souls to the Lord is the same task as winning nations to the Empire.

The Christian in the local situation is called upon to be a good citizen and to support both Empire and church in reaching and overcoming the pagan outside the Empire.

This new relationship between church and Empire changed the structures and form of mission immeasurably. The commitment of the ordinary person to the Lord undergirded the structures of society that strengthened and enlarged the Empire. Several dimensions of that change are important:

1) The unity of sacred and secular

Within the Empire there could be no distinction between sacred and secular. Bishops were leaders in things we might call secular (raising and deploying armies and playing major political roles, largely as stabilizing forces); kings and princes were leaders in things we might call religious (calling religious convocations and influencing their theological outcomes, just as the Emperor Constantine did at the Council of Nicea in 325).

2) Mission as a far off enterprise

Because the mission field by definition was outside the empire, mission became a task of foreign policy. Therefore, the initiative for enlarging church and Empire became the task of princes and armies, of missionary orders and missionary heroes and heroines. Mission was no longer the direct responsibility of the ordinary person. The world hostile to the Gospel was the pagan world way over there, beyond the boundary of the Empire. The Empire had the responsibility for reaching out to the pagan world, to incorporate it into Christendom by conquest. The Empire also had a responsibility to protect the church from the "infidel" who would subjugate the church to the service of a false god. Imperialism and mission, in this paradigm, were inseparable. Because we in the twentieth century have come to see the former as one of the Bad Things of history, we have a hard time recognizing that the connection between imperialism and mission was inevitable. In its origins, it was driven by a profound commitment to be faithful to God's command. Imperialism, bad as we now see much of it to have been, was seen as identical with the mission of the church. "Onward Christian Soldiers," the marching song of nineteenth century imperialism, expresses the sentiment perfectly. If it embarrasses us today, it is because the Christendom Paradigm no longer works for us.

3) Congregation as parish

Under the Christendom Paradigm, the local incarnation of church stopped being a tight community of convinced, committed, embattled believers supporting each other within a hostile environment. Instead, it became a parish, comprising a geographic region and all the people in it.

Everyone within the geographic bounds of the parish became *ipso facto* members of parish and church. No place in the local arena was seen as "outside" the church. All institutions (e.g., labor guilds, schools, merchant groups) understood themselves as manifestations of a unified existence—at once religious and secular. The parish pastor became a community chaplain, a civil servant, and local holy person.

4) The drive for unity

The vastness of the Empire/church demanded a kind of administration and cohesiveness that the church, at least, had not needed under the Apostolic Paradigm. For the whole thing to be managed it had to be unified. To assure unity in administration, theology, and politics, discord had to be minimized and standard structures developed. There was no space for differences. Ironically, it was this part of the paradigm that eventually began to pull apart, beginning in the break of the East from the West in 1053, gradually taking shape in the era of nationalisms and the national churches of the Reformation, and culminating finally in the denominational cacaphony of American religious life.[1]

In Christendom there could be only one church within one political entity. To be *outside* that unity was unthinkable, impossible. To be outside the faith was to be outside the law and the community. Heresy and treason were two sides of the same thing. In such a paradigm people who were disloyal to the faith or the nation could be tortured, oppressed, or killed precisely because they were profoundly "other"; to be fully a human being was to be a Christian and a member of the Empire. To be outside either was to be outside the law—an "outlaw."

5) The religious role of the laity

The ordinary person did not join the church as a matter of will, but as a matter of birth; to be born into the parish was by definition to become a part of community and church. Baptism recognized what was already a reality. The life of the entire community was understood as the medium for nurturing the individual in the faith; community pageants and festivals told the story of the faith; the educational system was also the religious system; the legal system defined and enforced the moral code of the faith.

6) The calling of the lay person

The ordinary person had a responsibility as a Christian to do some well-defined things: to be a good, law-abiding citizen; to pay the taxes that supported religious and secular institutions alike; to support the efforts to enlarge the Empire and bring in the pagan world; to be obedient to one's superiors (disobedience was both seditious and heretical); and to support the whole system with one's prayers and, if necessary, one's life.

In spite of the flaws we see in it now, the Christendom Paradigm had inner consistency. It made sense of life, though at the cost of oversimplifying it. But for the Christian, it cut the nerve of personal involvement and responsibility for witness and mission. That personal engagement was replaced with a sense of vicarious participation in a far-off mission carried out by heroes of the faith and armies of the nation-empire. It was difficult to see the ordinary folk of the village as a communion of the saints. Instead, the village became a support system for the saints of the mission, an outpost that sent CARE packages to the *real* mission.

A major difficulty of the Christendom Paradigm was its assumption that there was *one* answer, *one* way. Unfortunately, although the paradigm demanded uniformity, no lasting way was found to achieve it. For centuries ecumenical councils struggled to define the one statement that all could accept about various important matters of faith. But the one way was perpetually defeated by differences of opinion and conviction, and no way was found to enforce uniformity.

Loyalty and obedience were the primary virtues. But what to do about disloyalty and disobedience? The organizational implication of Christendom was a necessarily infallible hierarchy (where there is unity there can be no discord and therefore no error) with sacred and secular power united in one institution. That dream remains alive today for some in the religious world, and it undergirds the power of that religious-secular state, the Vatican.

Peculiarly enough, when the unity of life in Empire and church began to come apart, the Christendom Paradigm did not die. Instead, it continued to shape each of the fragments into which the world and the church broke. In Europe, today, for example, the Christendom Paradigm persists in each state (or provincial) church. The Church of England acted as if the English state and the English church were one, the parish system remained, and the Christendom Paradigm was perpetuated as an English myth in the English colonies.

Within what eventually became the United States, the shattered Christendom Paradigm produced denominational shards, each of which perpetuated something of the paradigm within its own boundaries. There was a make-believe quality in each shard's assumption that its world was a microcosm of the whole world of which it was the remnant, as if nothing else exits.

We will discuss other dimensions of the breakup of the paradigm later. For now I want to highlight the basic outline of the Christendom Paradigm and the strange way it fragmented at the end, with each fragment trying to continue to believe that it itself embodied the totality of the paradigm *(See Figure 3.)*

To describe this paradigm is to recognize that it never did reflect reality, nor does it seem very real to us today. It bespeaks a medieval world view with which we have many problems.

The paradigm's importance for us lies in the fact that most of the generation that now leads our churches grew up with it as a way of thinking about church and society. And all the structures and institutions that make up the churches and the infrastructure of religious life, from missionary societies to seminaries, from congregational life to denominational books of order and canons, are built on the presuppositions of the Christendom Paradigm—not the ancient, classical version of the paradigm as it was understood centuries ago, but the version that flourished with new life in the nineteenth and early twentieth centuries. This paradigm in its later years flourished and shaped us with new vigor, just as a dying pine is supposed to produce seed more vigorously as it senses the approach of its own death.

We are surrounded by the relics of the Christendom Paradigm, a paradigm that has largely ceased to work. But the relics hold us hostage to the past and make it difficult to create a new paradigm that can be as compelling for the next age as the Christendom Paradigm has been for the past age.

The final generations of the Christendom Paradigm have changed its six distinctive characteristics significantly, and all in today's churches have been deeply influenced by these changes.

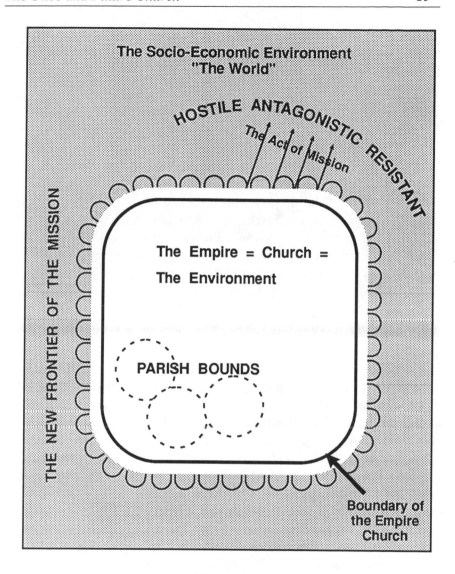

Figure 3

1) The unity of sacred and secular

Although our Constitution mandates a severe separation of church and state, in fact our nation has lived its own version of the Christendom Paradigm. An informal but fully operational religious establishment has held sway from the beginning—a creature of custom, never of law. National leaders have always been semi-religious figures. In the colonial years we experienced a confederated establishment of Congregational/ Presbyterian/Episcopal leadership. The political and social pressure to live out the Christendom Paradigm led to a kind of cultural religion that pledges quasi-religious allegiance to flag and country. Religious people and institutions experience much grief when they challenge this part of the Christendom Paradigm by criticizing government policy. Such rebelliousness violates the sense of what is right and proper for those who grew up under the Christendom Paradigm. Thus, the emergence of the "Moral Majority" among conservative Christians in the 1970s and 1980s represented an attempt not to replace the Christendom paradigm, but to substitute a conservative religious Christendom for a liberal one.

2) Mission as a far off enterprise

Mission to those far-off in pagan lands became an immensely powerful motivating and organizing factor for the churches in the nineteenth and twentieth centuries. Denominations organized themselves as missionary societies and their budgets were subscribed and oversubscribed because the people of the churches understood the priority of the missionary frontier. The clarity of the mission drove the pledging of the people. Local and regional groups organized to support that far-off mission. Education in churches was missionary education primarily, not theological education (education in matters of the faith and of the Scriptures was the function of the public school in reality, even though this contradicted the law). National bureaucracies and national buildings were structured to educate for mission and to administer mission—far away, primarily. The churches' concern for those in far-off lands continued to be connected with the nation's own sense of mission, i.e., the obligation to spread democracy (in a new manifestation of Empire) around the world. Imperialism and mission, born of the same paradigm, could not easily be separated.

3) Congregations as parish[2]

Local churches—particularly "mainline" ones—saw themselves as having territory or turf. Pastors felt themselves to be chaplains to an area, having a care for all the people, but a special care for those who "belonged" to the congregations. They tended to feel an obligation to "do" the children brought to them for baptism and the young couples brought to be married, without much thought to the religious preparation required. Those presenting themselves for membership were considered to have been converted already: membership classes were primarily orientation to a denomination's tradition. The ministry was carried out and controlled by the clergy. Because many denominations saw trained theological leadership as critical to the strength of its parishes, seminaries were invented and developed as special ways of building a professional cadre who could lead the churches. Indeed, the first institutions of higher education founded on these shores were begun primarily to meet the need for trained clergy.

4) The drive for unity

Each religious body or national church had a great sense of the oneness of the church and its mission, as if there were no others. Liturgies and theologies varied, yet people yearned for the certainties, the uniformity the Christendom Paradigm represented. The sense of difference disturbed many in church and state. For some, the differences led to feuds or strong competition for converts. In time the breakup of the unity began to lead some to attempts to rebuild an ecumenical entity and others to a firm loyalty to their own part of the truth. The overwhelming reality, however, was diversity and difference, not unity and coherence. The ecumenical bodies dedicated to unity never were as strong as the diverse alternatives. Indeed, the councils of churches have grown older, and they have grown weaker.

5) The religious place of the laity

Lay persons in the late period of the Christendom Paradigm continued to be seen as the loyal citizens of the realm, expected to be obedient to the powers, to pay their dues to church and state, and not to bother their heads too much about theological matters. They were expected to have a strong faith and a sense of commitment that they caught from the social institutions—the schools, the social groups, the community festivals. Those presenting themselves for membership were taught to be good citizens and loyal to their denominations. The lay person was not expected to have much to say or do about mission, except to support it vigorously with prayer, with generous giving, and by encouraging the young to go into "full-time Christian service" (meaning as an employee of the denomination, preferably overseas).

6) The calling of the laity

The ministry of the lay person was identical with being a good, law-abiding, tax-paying, patriotic citizen. One was to work hard and be obedient to the structures, institutions, and leaders of the community. One's sacred duty was to preserve the way things were and to avoid personal immorality, disloyalty, or diobedience to constituted authority. The Episcopal Prayer Book described the responsibility in these words: "to keep one's hands from picking and stealing." One's place in life was understood to be ordained by God, and one did not seek to change it lightly.

The Time between Paradigms

Nurtured in this fractionating Christendom paradigm and living within institutions shaped by it, we have begun to awaken to the early stages of a new one. Neither the new age nor the new paradigm has arrived, so we are pulled by the new and constrained by the old without the privilege even of knowing fully what the new will be like. But as the new has begun to reveal itself, it has made us profoundly uncomfortable.

In Thornton Wilder's classic *Our Town*, the young wife Emily dies in childbirth. Given the right to return to some special day of her life, she goes back to a birthday she remembers as a child. When she returns she sees her familiar loved ones going about their ordinary routines, but they cannot see her nor do they see the terrible beauty visible to her from beyond the grave. She flees, glad to return where the pain is at least bearable.

Wilder has given us a portrayal of what it is like to have awakened into a new paradigm and how hard it is to communicate with those still living in the old one. Emily could not stand the pain. Many younger Christians today may be suffering a similar painful dichotomy—being

born into a new paradigm and unable to communicate with those of us
who inhabit the old, they may be running away from the pain.

Our situation may be even more desperate than Emily's. More and
more we have lost our home in the familiar paradigm of Christendom,
but we have no clarity about how to find a new home in the turbulence of
the emerging world. The fault lines run through our own hearts.

William Willimon and Stanley Hauerwas describe their own experience of living in the earlier paradigm this way:

> You see, our parents had never worried about whether we would
> grow up Christian. The church was the only show in town. On
> Sundays, the town closed down. One could not even buy a gallon of
> gas. There was a traffic jam on Sunday mornings at 9:45, when all
> went to their respective Sunday schools. By overlooking much that
> was wrong in that world—it was a racially segregated world, re-
> member—people saw a world that looked good and right . . .Church,
> home, and state formed a national consortium that worked together
> to instill "Christian values." People grew up Christian simply by
> being lucky enough to be born in places like Greenville, South
> Carolina or Pleasant Grove, Texas.[3]

Then, humorously, they describe the day the paradigm began to die
for them:

> When and how did we change? Although it may sound trivial, one
> of us is tempted to date the shift sometime on a Sunday evening in
> 1963. Then, in Greenville, South Carolina, in defiance of the state's
> time-honored blue laws, the Fox Theater opened on Sunday. Seven
> of us—regular attenders of the Methodist Youth Fellowship at
> Buncombe Street Church—made a pact to enter the front door of the
> church, be seen, then quietly slip out of the back door and join John
> Wayne at the Fox.
>
> That evening has come to represent a watershed in the history of
> Christendom, South Carolina style. On that night, Greenville, South
> Carolina—the last pocket of resistance to secularity in the Western
> world—served notice that it would no longer be prop for the church
> . . . The Fox Theater went head to head with the church over who
> would provide the world view for the young. That night in 1963, the
> Fox Theater won the opening skirmish.[4]

The Christendom Paradigm probably began losing its power centuries ago. Willimon and Hauerwas describe the change in 1963—when, as they put it, "the Fox theater opened on Sunday . . . in defiance of the state's time-honored blue laws." Each inhabitant of a waning Christendom probably remembers a similar moment when the old way was irrevocably challenged and broken. But the break actually became unavoidable with the invention of an idea and a phrase—"ministry of the laity," which represents a change of consciousness. It recognizes the death of the old way, in which the laity had no direct call to ministry. Every time that phrase "ministry of the laity" is used, at that moment it is a little like the opening of the Fox theater on a Sunday evening in Greenville, South Carolina.

"Ministry of the laity" is a cliche today, so routine that it's almost boring. Nobody questions it. Everybody understands that it is a Good Thing. It is also true that very few people seem to have much grasp of it and very little is consciously done about it in the denominations—other than talk about how important and good it is. For these and other reasons, it is hard today to recognize the revolutionary meaning in the phrase. Under the Christendom Paradigm no one would have thought to talk about ministry of the laity. People did talk about "the priesthood of all believers" as a theological concept, but except for some experiments of the Reformation (and even there, Milton noted that "new presbyter is but old priest writ large"), no one seemed to take seriously that the ordinary Christian person was called on to be anything other than simply a law-abiding citizen.

In spite of its familiarity to us, the ministry of the laity is very new in the church. I have found no use of the phrase prior to the late 1930s. The first great book about it in English was Hendrik Kraemer's *Theology of the Laity* in 1958 (Yves Congar's *Jalons pour une Theologie du Laicat* [*Staking Out a Theology of the Laity*] had appeared five years earlier). The 1930s, 1953, 1958 were only yesterday in the life of an institution that measures change in generations and centuries. It is a brand new idea still—an idea yet to have its full impact on us.

It is hard for us who are so used to it to grasp its radical character. The phrase itself breaks new ground. The first revolutionary thing the phrase says is that "a lay person" is not the same as "a citizen." That is brand new. If laity have ministry, then a Christian who is a doctor or teacher or laborer has something special that they are called to do or say or—that word again—witness to in their world. Someone who has a ministry has a citizenship with God that may conflict with citizenship in a particular political state.

There it is. If there is a ministry of the laity, then the church is no longer the same as the Empire. Somehow the world, the nation, the environment is no longer the same as the church. The former understanding no longer holds true. In some new way we are conscious of the world as separate from, different from the church.

The change in language is simple, but its implications are vast. First, we can no longer assume that everybody is a Christian. Everybody has not been Christian for a long, long time, but our Christendom assumption has not changed. We ask Christian clergy to preach baccalaureate sermons, for example, ignoring the fact that many in the graduating class are not Christians. We now have to deal with the fact that in any geographic area the majority of people may have no interest in the church whatever. Congregation has forever separated from parish.

Second, people no longer assume that the community is a unit of the religious world, living out values derived from the Gospel. A new assumption has appeared, that something needs to be done to make a community "right" or "better." Further, it is assumed that the Christian who lives in a community has some responsiblity for doing something about it.

Third, we are returning to one of the features of the Apostolic Age. We now assume that the front door of the church is a door into mission territory, not just a door to the outside. Everybody who goes through that door is personally crossing a missionary frontier and is involved in mission. This hearkening back to the Apostolic Age has an important qualifier, however, as we shall see.

Every one of those assumptions violates the mind-set of the Christendom Paradigm. Indeed, under the impact of such new assumptions the Christendom Paradigm is coming apart at the seams. All the institutions and patterns of life that grew up during Christendom are having their foundations shaken.

The crisis for congregations, Christians, and those who care about the Gospel is that the outlines of the new paradigm are not yet clear. Tested landmarks have disappeared, but we still lack enough clarity to know what new landmarks we need, much less how to find or fashion them. Indeed, it may be that the new paradigm may never become as compelling as either the Apostolic or the Christendom versions. The new paradigm may call for more diversity than we are used to or comfortable with.

Let us illustrate what we do see about the emerging paradigm:

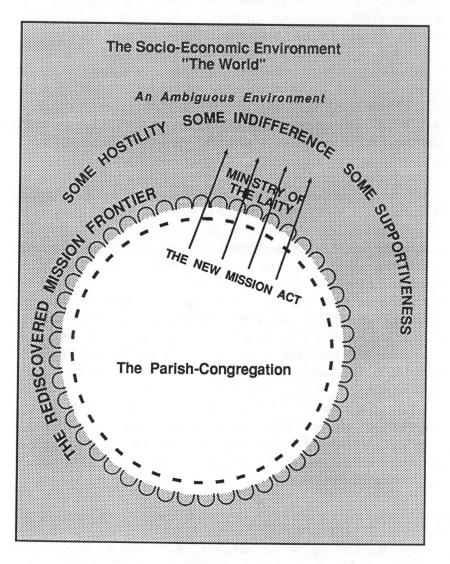

Figure 4

Note in Figure 4 the reappearance of the missionary frontier close-in to the congregation. The difference between this and Figure 1 is important, although here we note that the environment is "ambiguous."

How we read the environment, as we have seen above, says a lot about how the church sees itself and its mission. In Figure 2 the environment was hostile, leading the church to form tight congregations of people with high commitment. In Figure 3, the church sees itself as identified with the environment. Its perimeters are geographic, not boundaries of intent and commitment. In Figure 4 the environment beyond the boundary is "ambiguous." It is not always hostile, although sometimes it is. It is not identical with the church, although sometimes it still is. Much that is in the environment is somewhere in between; the school systems, for example, attempt to teach truth and justice, but disconnected from their roots in the biblical witness.

The outside boundary of the congregation is porous and permeable, as in the time of Christendom. People move in and out with little sense of responsibility for mission and little knowledge of what the congregation is all about. The culture that used to pretend to teach faith no longer does so, but the congregation has not discovered patterns and disciplines for nurturing either its people or newcomers to the faith.

A very uncertain congregation, then, looks across an unfamiliar missionary frontier to an environment that appears less and less friendly and wonders. It often discovers that ambiguities from the environment have migrated into the congregation itself. It wonders how to constitute itself for the new mission that the new world calls for. It wonders what good news it has, how to deliver it, and to whom. It wonders how to differentiate itself from its environment. It does not know how to deal with environmental ambiguity in its own life and values.

At the same time, some members of the congregation see the shift in ages and paradigms and struggle to discover a better way. Right beside those persons in almost every congregation are some still living in the Christendom Paradigm, unaware of the changed age and unwilling to let go of the familiar past.

Summary

The church has always worked out its self-understanding and ordered its internal life in dialogue with the world that surrounded it. Its sense of mission has provided the energy for its life, shaping the roles and relationships in its institutions. Where a sense of mission has been clear and compelling, the church has been sacrificial and heroic in its support of that mission.

Within the Apostolic Paradigm, the church formed itself in strong local entities or congregations and nurtured its people to reach out to a hostile environment to witness to the good news of the biblical story and of Jesus. There was diversity and pluriformity in the roles and relationships as shaped by local conditions, reinforced by a real effort to maintain effective linkages to congregations in other places.

The second great way of being church—the Christendom Paradigm—was born, flourished, and began its decline during the last millennium and a half. Here the identity of church shifted in response to a new understanding of how it should relate to its environment. Because the Empire was by definition identical with the church, and because the world outside the Empire was seen as a pagan environment, mission moved far away. Because the missionary frontier became the same as the Empire's frontier, to be a citizen was to be a churchman. The local congregation, previously characterized by high commitment and training in the faith, now became a geographic region within which institutions of society and government were assumed to support the faith and religious institutions were enlisted in the aims of society and government. In the end, mission became the responsibility of the professionals.

The third way of being church has begun to be born, but its birth is not complete. Once again the church and the individual person of faith are beginning to discover a sense of a new mission frontier. But that frontier has not yet become clear or compelling enough; we see the horizon, but the path we must follow remains obscure. Worse, the church's energy for mission today is conflicted and at war with itself.

It is also true that the forms and structures, the roles and relationships of the churches we have inherited were formed by paradigms that no longer work for us. We live in the memory of great ways of understanding how to be church and to be in mission. Those memories surround us like ruins of an ancient civilization. Our educational institutions and our structures of leadership and service are likewise conflicted and at war with themselves.

How do we build religious institutions within which we can live out our calling to serve the world? How do we form ourselves for mission to the emerging age?

These may be our questions for the next age.

NOTES

1. Members of the historic "free" churches had experiences that distanced them from the full impact of the Christendom Paradigm. My appendix chapter describes the different dynamics of that paradigm. But *even* in those churches the Christendom Paradigm had powerful influence, particularly in their second and third generations.

2. Again, I refer to the somewhat different experience of the Free Church tradition as noted in the Appendix.

3. Stanley Hauerwas and William H. Willimon, *Resident Aliens* (Nashville: Abingdon, 1990, p. 16).

4. Ibid., pp. 15-16.

CHAPTER III

Cracks in the Systems

Systems that seem stable and secure often have internal tensions and pressures that lead to dramatic, surprising changes. Most western Europeans and others were aware of what seemed to be monolithic, powerful governments in the communist East during 1988 and 1989. When the Berlin Wall came down, incredulous Westerners could hardly accept the evidence of their eyes.

In the aftershock, wise people have been able to point out the signs of change that were there earlier, but most of us did not see them. In fact, the walls and governments of the East seem now to have been a fragile facade. The people of the East had long ceased to believe in them and honor them. The stability and security of the structures were fictional. As I note in Chapter V, this particular illustration may say a lot about changes in our denominational systems.

Cicadas know something about that. They grasp tree bark as they feel growth and change within themselves, then burst out of the old, unchanged carapace, leaving it hanging lifeless on the tree. They fly away. Geologists tell us that deep below the surface of the earth are immense tectonic plates upon which the continents ride, shifting slowly but with immense force across the globe. Fault lines mark the boundaries where these plates touch. As the continents shift, enormous tension and energy builds up until with the lurch of an earthquake the tension is relieved for the time being. There isn't much you can *do* about a fault line, but if you know it's there and you cannot stand anxiety, you can choose to move somewhere else. Or you can learn to construct buildings to take into account the special conditions of unstable ground.

Changes as radical as those the church is experiencing as the age of Christendom disintegrates cause severe dislocations in some parts of the religious world, even while there may be no sense of movement or even tension elsewhere. For some there is the chaos of daily earthquakes; for others there is a sense that nothing much has changed and the earth does not move.

Changes of paradigm are, by definition, matters of perception, feeling, world view, consciousness; they are not external changes like the levelling of a mountain. As a result, one of the most difficult realities we deal with is the fact that two people, living side by side, may face the same phenomenon, yet their perceptions may differ radically. Even worse, one individual may see part of reality through the Christendom Paradigm and the rest of life in quite a different way. She or he may not even feel the fault line running through such behavior.

Al, a Presbyterian pastor, told me of a frustrating conflict he had with an elder when he tried to promote an antiwar initiative in his congregation when our national leaders were proposing confrontation with Iraq in the Persian Gulf. The elder was angry. She fought Al tooth and nail. "But the funny thing was," Al told me, "I couldn't get her to talk about 'war' and 'peace'; she simply was convinced that it was disloyal and wrong to question government policy." Al said, "She didn't blow up and quit the church until I said, 'The government's policy is immoral, and the church has got to stand up against it.'"

When I asked what the elder said in response, Al told me, "I am disappointed that my pastor would be disloyal to my country. I was brought up to believe in God and country and will not go along with what you are saying." Al reduced the problem to a political disagreement, but I saw an elder holding up the values of another paradigm— that the Empire and the church are one. Al had so much at stake in the political issue that he did not hear where his elder was coming from.

In that anecdote two ages were talking past each other. The elder saw the governing order as ordained by God, and that it was the task of the Christian to support the government at the same time that one worked to improve it. She couldn't conceive of the church as opposed to the Empire. She *could*, however, probably see the need to vote for another administration. But *oppose* the government? Heresy! Treason! Both.

Al, on the other hand, spoke out of the emerging paradigm or age in which one must make careful discriminations between those initiatives of government that serve the Gospel and those that are opposed to the Gospel. Al, as a matter of fact, was pretty extreme himself. *He* couldn't

consider or even conceive of how the Empire sometimes can and does
serve the Gospel.

I felt both were missing the boat and *needed* to be able to hear and
affect each other's thinking. Neither the elder nor Al was willing to go
beyond pre-set positions. Both were stuck in their own paradigms,
unable to see or hear the other.

When paradigms shift, our battles get as confusing as the one between Al and his elder. Antagonists can argue past each other, fight each
other because they do not realize that they are standing in different
paradigms. That is why going to a regional denominational meeting can
be a modern equivalent of visiting the Tower of Babel.

What *I* hear is people—clergy and laity—talking the same language,
using the same words, but totally misunderstanding each other. Indeed,
the speakers do not even speak consistently from the same worldview.
The understanding of each has been shaped, more or less, by the worldview of Christendom. That worldview also shapes how they understand
their roles and the church's role in society.

At the same time, each has been affected by the new age's consciousness of ministry and mission. Each is pulled in both directions.
Miscommunication is to be expected!

It is therefore important to pay attention to the places where dislocations are occurring, where the tectonic plates are shifting between the
two ages.

Most dislocations are occurring around the fault lines, and it is there
that clear communication is most difficult. When pain and discomfort
develop and when they lead to conflict, people living in different paradigms perceive the trouble differently and see different implications
about what to do.

Today, there are four arenas of real dislocation in the way religious
systems are operating: the role of the clergy, the role of the laity, that of
the bishop or executive, and that of the congregation.

The Role of the Clergy

In the Christendom Paradigm, the role of clergy was clear. It was strong,
central, and unquestioned. It was a high-status role, carrying authority.
Clergy were *the ministry*.

Clergy were chaplains and guarantors of community life, with power far beyond the walls of the church. As a thirty-year-old Episcopal priest walking the streets of a village in southern England, I often had mayor and street-sweeper alike defer to me as "Rector." Their deference was not to me, but to the power the pastor carried in Christendom. For many people in churches today, that remains a very attractive idea. For many people the problem would be solved if we could return to that strong, hierarchical model, when Herr Pastor was Herr Pastor and The rector was truly the "ruler" (which is what the word meant in Latin).

The network of clergy, operating within their strong, clear role at the center of the church's institutional life, built a formidable power system, designed to provide strong and consistent leadership of the institution for its mission. But the power the clergy gained was well-nigh impregnable. Aidan Kavanaugh, the Roman Catholic liturgical scholar, speaks of that power as "the hegemony of the presbyterate." That coalition of power in clergy hands was a fact in denominations regardless of their polities. The Free Churches fought against it more than those who had roots in the establishments, with Brethren and Quakers more consistently successful.

The fossils of that hegemony from the Christendom Paradigm make up much of the power system that rules religious institutions today, making change very difficult to effect. Its name is clericalism.

Clericalism—like sin—is carrying a good thing too far. The clear role and authority given to the ordained leader really did and often still does facilitate the mission of the church. But the development of the clergy into a special class with special privilege and considerable power to govern a large institution is what Kavanaugh's phrase points to. Regardless of the polity of the denomination, it is my impression that clergy have, effectively, a veto on every important issue. If they genuinely believe a course of action is wrong, it will not happen.

But the hegemony of the presbyterate, the all-powerful authority of the clergy as a class, is breaking down. Most church members, even clergy, welcome that fact, but they find the resulting arrangements to be confusing and chaotic. Hegemony was authoritarian and clericalist, but it *was* predictable. It is sometimes hard to know "who's on first" now that hegemony is disappearing. It is also surprising how the power of clericalism continues to influence and rule even as the paradigm changes. It is far from dead!

Along this fault line individual clergy have much less clarity about who they are and what their roles are. The reappearance of the frontier of mission on the church's doorstep has shifted mission responsibility more and more onto the shoulders of the laity, bringing their role to new prominence and power. Most clergy agree that that is right and good. At the same time, this shift has undercut the previously accepted role of the clergy. Consequently many clergy are double-minded: they give lip service to the ministry of the laity in the pulpit on Sunday, but jealously guard their prerogatives throughout the week and especially in denominational planning groups.

Many clergy are searching for roles that are clearer and less ambiguous. Some see themselves as social activists or spiritual directors, "enablers" or community organizers, educators or counselors. In some cases these new role descriptions are added onto the more traditional roles of preacher, pastor, and administrator. Without clear grounding, however, some clergy find themselves flipping back and forth, chasing roles as if they were fads. One man, whom I first knew in the 1950s, was then a pastor-educator. Next I heard, he was a pastor-counselor. Then followed in rapid succession human relations trainer, community organizer, consultant, renewalist, and most recently a spiritual director. I'm eager to see what comes next.

This loss of role clarity lies behind much of the stress and burnout among clergy. Most clergy come to their vocations from a deep faith and commitment. Trained in institutions that were generated by the mind-set of Christendom and ordained into denominations and congregations predominately shaped by Christendom, they discover that the rules have been changed in the middle of the game. Instead of being front-line leaders and spokespersons for mission, they now feel they are being asked to take a back seat to a newly awakened laity. The role they sought out and trained themselves for no longer fits what they have to do. Many are unsure how to give leadership in the new time.

The loss of power and role clarity sometimes causes depression, anger, and grief among clergy, making them more likely to seek scapegoats in "the seminaries," "the bishop," "lay people," or "the national church." Many clergy I know are bitter and angry at how the church has misused them, as they see it.

There is another important side to this. The clergy, as manager-leaders of the *institution*, badly need laity to help lead and support the institution (raise money, lead program, etc.). Clergy I know are already torn because they know institutional needs interfere with the genuine call of laity to be primarily engaged in family, job, and community. The result? Many clergy are painfully ambivalent—even schizophrenic—about what they want the laity to be and do. If they really succeed in getting laity invested in the mission frontier, it will disrupt the operation of the parish.

The Role of the Laity

The overwhelming majority of lay people in congregations 30 years ago understood what was expected of them. One of my senior wardens put it to me this way about thirty-five years ago: "My job is to back you up. Make sure the parish budget is raised and balanced. Make sure we're doing our part for the diocese and the mission program. Beyond that— my job is to keep my nose clean, pay my taxes, do my job, not run around, keep the booze under control, and support the governor and the president, especially if he's a Democrat!" Simple. Clear. Many lay people continue to understand their own ministry that way—most of the time.

But today the lay church member receives another set of messages, not all of which are consistent. These become points of stress and change as the paradigm shifts:

a. The lay Christian is told to support the parish with tithes of time, talent, and treasure. She or he is asked about this regularly and recruited to do things in organizations of the congregation, which, even in a small congregation, are many. The system makes a lot of noises that suggest the faithful member ought to be doing more than is usually the case.

b. The rhetoric from the pulpit urges engagement with the world and defines one's "real" ministry as job, community life, family, etc., all of which take place *outside* the church. Yet the bulletin, the parish organization, the pastor, and staff urge and reward engagement with parish *activities*. Ministry outside the church is rarely recognized and never rewarded. Ministry inside *is* recognized and rewarded. The pastoral calling that is done is generally done in homes, not in the work-place. Assignments to responsibilities in the congregation are generally made according to the congregation's organizational needs, not the expertise of the lay person. What is *said* at church undergirds the new paradigm. What is *done* tends to reflect assumptions left over from the Christendom Paradigm.

c. The lay person is often urged by the pastor to take positions on a series of complex, emotional issues (abortion, the civil rights of gays and lesbians, premarital sex, divorce, South Africa, war and peace). Generally the pastor advocates one position as "the" Christian position and provides educational opportunities supportive of that position. The lay member can be deeply distressed if she or he disagrees. Often there is no honorable space for disagreement. Passions and resentments may run deep.

d. The lay person hears of actions of the national or regional church on controversial issues. Sometimes he or she finds it hard to understand why the church is so focused on those particular issues and seems to ignore the things one was "brought up" to think to be important. Why worry about economic justice and seem not to care about divorce or premarital sex? Why get involved with foreign affairs when our children don't know the Bible? It is right to care for hungry people, but what right has the church to talk about agricultural policy or employment training programs? The lay person who brings up questions like these is often put on the defensive by clergy who seem more intent on winning an argument than helping their members make connections. The denomination's educational materials may reflect a paradigm that is out of touch with the paradigm the member lives in.

e. Lay persons sometimes do not understand why cherished parts of their religious past—worship forms, hymns, congregational customs and practices—need to be changed. People have a sense that they have no power in the decisions about those changes. Indeed, they sometimes feel that their strong concerns about those cherished parts of the past are ridiculed and denigrated by clergy and denominational leaders.

f. Although some articulate lay leaders today call for laity to be the primary ministers of the church, neither clergy nor laity are clear what that means. As a matter of fact, most lay people are already doing what they assumed they were supposed to do—working hard in their jobs and trying to make their communities better. They are surprised and hurt to find that their leaders consider those expressions of faithfulness somehow wanting. Indeed, committed laity sometimes feel their efforts in ministry are disparaged by church leaders. They feel patronized by the ordained. Many such lay persons really do not know what else is expected of them. All too many laity, nurtured in the Christendom Paradigm, simply have backed away from the painful experiences that continually face them at church.

If the clergy in the emerging age feel a sense of schizophrenia in understanding and fulfilling their role, so do the laity.

The Role of Bishop or Church Executive

Just as the roles of clergy and laity have become more problematical, the bishops and other denominational executives who serve in the regional office of the denomination feel the changes even more. Although different denominations have different names for these roles (bishop, superintendent, executive, general minister, area minister, etc.) each bears responsibility for what St. Paul described as "the care of all the churches." They function as coordinators, supporters, judges, spiritual guides, leaders, managers, chief pastors, teachers, and administrators. Their offices are the first place local congregations and pastors go when something goes wrong. The very real differences in the authority these roles carry from one denomination to another should not blind us to the very large areas of similarity between how they actually function.

Until now, the revolution in ministry has affected primarily clergy and laity. Judicatory[1] leaders *so far* have been affected by the change of ministry age in two ways: (1) They have received increased calls to intervene when clergy-lay friction erupts into a bruising battle, which happens frequently in these times of confused and conflicting roles and (2) they must deal with almost annual reductions in resources in regional budgets. Congregations genuinely trying to respond to the missionary frontier on their doorsteps naturally see a more convincing case to fund their own mission endeavor rather than support the judicatory. Both of these pressure points—the increase in congregation tensions and the decrease in resources—are more likely to increase than to decrease.

Few executives and bishops are aware that the new paradigm is threatening to marginalize further the role they played in the past. They have such increasing demands on them amid continually decreasing resources that few of them can focus on more than the here and now. As the old story tells it, it is hard to drain the swamp when you are surrounded by alligators nipping at you.

Once upon a time in Christendom, these executives had central leadership roles in the mission of the churches. They motivated, coordinated, shepherded the churches, and focused energy on building up a church for the far-off mission tasks. Their functions and practices were shaped for that task. They were our mission leaders. The excitement and energy that led to building national structures for denominations was fueled by Christendom's clarity about a far-off mission. National and regional structures proved themselves by their ability to bring individuals and congregations to participate sacrificially in mission beyond their borders.

But when congregations rediscovered a primary missionary frontier at their own doorstep, the judicatories did not seem to be as necessary; indeed, sometimes they seemed to be impediments. Congregations felt no need to ask the bishop before setting up a soup kitchen. Sometimes, as a matter of fact, they forgot to tell their executive that they had begun such a mission effort. The judicatory was seen as irrelevant to these strictly local expressions of mission.

I recently ran into a remarkable Lutheran congregation made up mostly of retired folk. They had carved out a special niche of ministry—doing laundry for one of the city's homeless shelters. I am not sure how they got started, but the effort is a very large one for them, and they are justifiably proud. When their bishop's assistant most recently visited to preach, he spent most of his time drumming up support for the capital funds drive to provide a camp and conference center for the synod. It seemed to the church members that the judicatory was only interested in funds to run itself and did not understand why a congregation might find its local mission effort more impelling. The people got the impression that their synod was not particularly interested in what they were trying to do in mission.

Unless judicatory leaders are able to shed this image and rediscover a central role in mission leadership, it is unlikely that they will again be as influential as they were in past generations. Christendom once gave them a central role because they were central to mission. In the new paradigm, they have been unable as yet to clarify their role, ground that role in the new mission frontier, or communicate a convincing case for a role in mission.

In many places loyalty to tradition and traditional patterns is strong and continues to support the denominations' systems and their bishops and executives. In other places those leaders, noting the erosion of traditional support, have responded by developing and marketing imaginative, often constructive, mission programs that attract both support and commitment. Imaginative marketing and programming cannot for long, however, obscure the need for a basic redirection of effort. The mission the judicatory has been most successful at defining is not the one that engages the people at the congregation's doorstep. What is worse, the mission the judicatory promotes most energetically looks more and more to congregations like the same old institutional baggage dressed up with new language.

The funding shortfalls in judicatory after judicatory are the logical result of what I am describing, and they have been getting worse for three decades. Although imaginative marketing, vigorous capital fund campaigns, staff reductions, and re-organizations can paper over the problem temporarily, the real concern is only postponed. People of the church will support what they understand to be mission. What they see coming from their denominational offices does not look like mission to them any more. No number of bishops and executives will convince them that it is a duck if it keeps on barking. The church's people *hear* quacking in other places and want help from the judicatory. They are not particularly interested in supporting systems that do not seem to help them very much with what they want to be working at—their mission.

I believe the church of the new age or paradigm is going to need strong effective leadership and skill from its judicatories. But judicatories designed for Christendom will not be sufficient for the new church.

I believe that the ministry role crisis, which has been so painful for clergy and confusing to laity over the past half-century, will, in the next generation, make the work of the denominational executive or bishop extraordinarily difficult. Some judicatory systems may not survive. Some national systems are already in serious trouble. A wise friend states the case more dramatically than I do: "It seems to me," he says, "that what God is doing right now is dismantling the denominational systems as fast as possible."

Action for mission has always driven people in the churches, whether or not they have a clear (or even right) target for their mission concern. Most congregations now see little connection between what their judicatory or denomination proposes as mission and what they themselves identify as mission. Fewer and fewer will find it compelling to support staffs and budgets they feel to be only marginally in touch with mission.

Despite these serious shortcomings, an important case remains to be made for the importance of judicatories within denominations. Potentially, they can still provide a wider view of mission, offer important challenge and support, provide connections to resources, and make available technical assistance for launching new ventures. Even more important is their role in providing a stable back-up system, just "being there" to help the congregation when it hits a bad patch or gets overwhelmed by an opportunity.

On the whole, they are not now making a convincing case to most congregations. Their increasing impotence is a serious matter for the health of all congregations.

The Role and Work of the Congregation

All the uncertainties and changes of the emerging age of ministry come to a head in the life of the local congregation. Once a stable center and guarantor of community and family life, it witnessed to the deep values and commitments that made life coherent and whole. Today, the local church has become merely one institution alongside all the others, competing for time and energy and often less sure than the others about its basic reason for being.

Clergy and laity alike struggle with two realities in congregations today:

1) It is harder and harder to maintain the congregational structure and systems that have served so many generations so well. The institutional framework of congregations is not working efficiently in many places. The financial system undergirding congregations is overwhelmed by rising costs and hemmed in by uneconomic assumptions about professional leadership and organizational structure. Clergy and lay leaders have overwhelmingly difficult tasks.

2) It is becoming clearer that urgent needs are calling for *more* caring ministries. *Every* congregation is faced with increasing needs for ministry on its doorstep. The need for imaginative, caring

ministries that reach out to the community is greater than ever. But both laity and clergy face the new challenge unclear about their roles and unclear about how to move ahead. In short, the *need* for strong congregations comes at the very time when congregations are most fragile and uncertain, and when their primary support system is threatened.

In this climate, many respond by trying harder and harder to do the old thing better. They try to turn the clock back to the familiar dream of the Christendom Paradigm, working to resurrect an antiquarian institution. I am reminded of an apocryphal church board whose members all died in a church fire because they could not figure out the proper way to use *Robert's Rules of Order* to adjourn the meeting.

A variation on this theme is the response of the evangelical, more conservative denominations and like-minded wings within liberal denominations. These groups seem to be trying to rebuild a Christendom that is a "holy club" of personal and family religious enthusiasm in, but not engaged with, the church's social environment. It responds to the mission frontier of the individual, but not of the community. This response arises in spite of the pioneering history of these groups, who were the first to perceive the gap between the demands of the gospel and the policies of the state in areas such as slavery and child labor.

Historically, the more liberal among and within the denominations were the last to recognize the gap between church and Empire. Their establishment roots made it difficult for them to differentiate between the values of state and society on the one hand and those of the Gospel on the other. Yet, once convinced of the problem, as I believe they were through the upheavals of the civil rights movement and Vietnam, liberal religious leaders seem to focus on building a liberal political realm in which theologians called the tune, a new Christendom where liberal theologians call the shots of the Empire.

The conservatives' much noted "great reversal" at the turn of the century led them from engagement with the world toward a Christendom of personal religion. The liberal "great reversal" half a century later led their elites—but not their people—toward a Christendom that looks for all the world like a liberal Empire, a secular version of Calvin's Geneva.

Some in both the liberal and conservative camps respond to the tension of role confusion and anxiety by buying into society's utilitarian

values. They design marketable churches and search for things that
"work." Ten steps to this and twelve dynamics of that. I am embar-
rassed that many of the purveyors of this line call themselves consultants; I find some of them hard to distinguish from snake-oil salesmen
flogging the latest miracle cure.

I speak harshly about these aberrations because I am attracted to
something in every one of them. Yet none does justice to the radical
demands of the new mission frontier; all are patchwork responses. I
believe that the discomfort of the congregation is a call to something
genuinely new.

Congregations—like clergy, laity, and executives—are living in a
time in which landmarks have been erased and old ways have stopped
working. We also live in a time when the answers have not yet become
clear. It is a time that calls for steadiness and perseverance through
uncertainty. Such a time generates energy for change, but it also generates intense anxiety that makes partial answers attractive, so long as they
are quick.

The church—its laity, clergy, congregations, executives, and bishops—has organized and structured itself for one mission. We have
awakened to a world in which the mission frontier has changed. The
organization and the structures of church life, formed for that one mission, now need to be reoriented to face the new frontier.

The task ahead is the reinvention of the church.

NOTE

1. "Judicatory" is one of those awful invented words that no one has been able to
get rid of or improve upon. I understand the Presbyterians inflicted it upon us, reflecting
as it does their understanding of levels of the denomination as different "courts." I will
use the word as infrequently as possible, primarily to denote the regional entity of a
denomination that relates to local congregations. Technically the word is used for any
entity of the denomination larger than the local congregation.

CHAPTER IV

The Reinvention of the Church

What does all this mean? It means that God who called the church out into the apostolic world two thousand years ago is again calling the church out, this time into a secularized world where its mission and its life must be once again redefined.

In the days of the formation of the Jesus movement, the forms of Mediterranean Hellenistic culture did not fit a people who had heard the radical Gospel of Jesus. The followers of the new way responded with close-knit community cells informally and loosely linked together. Centuries later those structures for that marginal religious movement proved inadequate for the official religion of a world empire. In that second calling out, the church was led to a structure of parishes within an imperial system.

For the most part, those forms have now stopped working. God is calling us out of them to systems that will support our life and mission for the coming age.

The dilemma of the church in this transitional time is that the shells of the old structures still surround us even though many of them no longer work. Some of the structures are institutions, some are roles, some are mind-sets and expectations. At one moment they mediate grace to us and at the next they block and confuse us. Sometimes some of them actually support and nourish us, while others get in the way of the new structures we need.

Our task is no less than the reinvention of the church. It may take several generations. We will not see the end of it, but we must begin now.

In this chapter, I want to talk about the reinvention as a process that will engage those of us who care about the church for the rest of our lives. In doing so, I will touch on three key polarities with which we will struggle and then identify some structural issues we will have to solve. I shall also note some resources for the task and some threats that lie ahead.

Three Polarities

By definition, polarities are differences you live with but never resolve. Polarities are particularly galling to religious people who want a clearly defined "right" and "wrong." But in fact, the history of the church is the story of many polarities. The catholic spirit and the protestant principle. The push toward the charismatic and the struggle for ordered life. The tension between law and grace, faith and works. Flesh and spirit. The elect and the nations. If there is a lesson from this history, it is that one is always tempted toward one of the poles, but that none of them is complete by itself. Fanaticism seems to be, almost by definition, the establishment of one pole as absolute truth and the absolute rejection of the polar opposite. Some polarities come into play as we think of reinventing the church for the next generations.

Parish vs. Congregation

The words "parish" and "congregation" reflect important meanings with deep roots in the church's experience. While the former was the dominant form of Christendom and the latter of the Apostolic age, the concepts are larger than either of these.

Parish means turf. Place. It includes within it a sense of the responsibility of the church for the people of the neighborhood, regardless of their relationship to the faith. Parish includes the farms and businesses within the area. It spreads over environmental, social, and economic relationships as well as personal, family, and moral concerns. The word stands for the fact that the church cannot separate itself from its social context, from realms of politics and economic life. It is engaged indissolubly with the world. The idea of parish also assumes close linkage to other parishes in a network of relationship.

At its best, parish stands for the church's commitment to serve and strengthen the fabric of the community and society. Its patron saint is Jeremiah who, when his Empire was crashing about his shoulders, went out to buy a field, grounding himself (literally) by showing he belonged to the land.

At its worst, parish signifies a comfortable accommodation between religious life and political forces. Parish understands what it means to be "at ease in Zion," accepting the protection of the state's powers by muting the cry for justice.

At the other pole of meaning is the concept "congregation." As parish focuses on turf, congregation focuses on people—believing, committed people. Congregation refers to those who choose to engage with and accept a life within the framework of faith. Where parish implies first a relationship to society, congregation implies first a separation from it. Congregation speaks to the need for a deep, nurturing religious community based on commitment and mutual support. More easily than parish, congregation can stand alone without depending on linkage to other congregations.

At best, congregation nurtures an intensity of faith-commitment that can result in personal, moral, and spiritual growth at the same time it impels individuals to minister to social ills. At best, congregation is able to recognize the injustices of the political realm, often because of the consequences to specific persons. At worst, congregation turns ingrown, fostering religiosity and narrow personal moralism. It becomes unwilling to bear the burdens of those outside the congregation. It can ignore the responsibility to build a just social order.

Jesus called upon the church to be "in, but not of" the world. Both parish and congregation at their best approach that high calling. Parish, however, leans toward the sin of being exclusively "in" the world; congregation is similarly tempted to be "not of" the world. We need parishes and congregations that are able to draw energy from both poles.

In the church we have to reinvent, these two polar realities will remain in tension. During the time of the Christendom Paradigm the predominant form was parish, although the reality of congregation was reaffirmed by the Reformation and through the Free Church tradition (see the appendix). Parish is the heritage of the mainline denominations, even those who call themselves congregational—those who have been close to the establishment. Congregation is the gift and heritage of the Free Church traditions.

In the reinvention the pendulum will swing toward congregation. In fact, a swing has already begun. The external linkage system of every parish has eroded significantly. The sense of responsibility for turf has been stunted as the shortfall of resources has made parish focus all too often on members more than mission.

In the pendulum's swing, we must preserve the best of what parish means and also seek to avoid the worst of what congregation has meant. It will not be enough to shore up what we have known as parish or as congregation. What is already at work is a difficult interpenetration of the two, an irresolvable tension of polarities, neither of which can be abandoned. What we need in the age to come is not parishes of civil religion or congregations of the righteous, but a new thing.

Servanthood vs. Conversion

A second polarity has to do with the church's understanding of what its mission is. This polarity is reflected in the two ways the church has described its work—conversion of the world or serving the world. Both terms are drawn directly from Jesus' ministry. He called his followers to go to the ends of the earth to convert, but he also sent his disciples to be servants even as he had been one who served them.

At no time has the church ordered its life exclusively to one or the other pole, although the predominant public model of both Apostolic and Christendom Paradigms was conversion. I note that as the public model, the one that drove the engines of the institution, although I suspect that the predominant private model has always been servanthood. Literally millions of ordinary folk have acted out their faith in caring for their neighbors and for those in pain around them, often without even thinking of it as mission.

Conversion, at its best, leads to bringing the stranger into life-giving relationship to the Gospel and to a nurturing community. It has always been an imperative laid upon those who follow Jesus. More than an imperative requirement, it has been the natural response of the believer, reaching out to share the source of his or her own new life.

At its least attractive, conversion has led past generations to religious and military imperialism. In our day the imperialism has been more likely that of psychological coercion and manipulation, all too often masked as crusades or evangelistic campaigns. My skeptical friends call it "religious scalp-hunting."

Servanthood, the other pole of mission, reflects the way Jesus lived as a servant among others. Millions have followed his example, giving their lives for others. Teachers, doctors and nurses, agricultural specialists, and engineers have expressed this meaning of mission across the world as they have given skill and insight into improving life for others. Ordinary folk have done ordinary caring things for those around them because of Jesus. The fruits of this servanthood are impressive—school systems around the world, health and medical systems, the ability of tribes and peoples to communicate with one another through taught language, and a growing world-wide consensus about the value of the individual's well-being.

Servanthood's temptation is not, like conversion's, to coerce and manipulate, but to lose its depth and grounding. It can degenerate into mere activism and "do-good-ism" when it loses its intimate link to the story and example of Jesus. The worst of servanthood is seen in the mindless bureaucracies that institutionalize good intentions without preserving the call to serve. It can be found as easily in church programming and institutions as in the public sector.

The local religious community of the future will have to move beyond the simplistic either/or we experience today. Servanthood vs. conversion is not a choice to be made; it is a polarity that must be built into the structures we create for the church.

Exclusive or Inclusive

A third polarity relates to the church's image of itself. Is it to be exclusive or inclusive? Is it to uphold tight, demanding criteria for membership or open its arms as wide as possible to bring in the stranger and sojourner? Both poles reflect important parts of the Christian heritage.

There is strong precedent within the church for strict enforcement of clearly stated boundaries. At times the boundaries are primarily moral (acceptable moral behavior), at times they are creedal (right belief according to specific belief statements); at times they can be tribal (belonging to the right group). Where there is a strong consensus about those standards, it is possible to assure considerable conformity. But where the standards cease to represent compelling inner convictions, the exclusive community collapses. "Temperance," for example, served as a strong behavioral boundary for religious groups such as the Methodists for decades. When lay leaders came to accept the fact that even some

Methodist pastors occasionally took a social drink, the moral boundary eroded. "Inerrancy" of Scripture still serves as a powerful boundary for many, but even some of them now wonder about the story of Jonah and the whale. The more they wonder, the less strong the boundary is. And the increasing stridency of those who support that boundary suggests increasing anxiety about it.

At its worst, exclusivity becomes rigid and legalistic, separating the righteous from the unrighteous according to manmade standards. (A friend has told me that one of the laws of religion is that "All people are divided into two groups—the righteous and the unrighteous; and the righteous usually do the dividing!")

But exclusivity is important because it speaks of something more important than these limited boundaries. Exclusivity states that there must be a place where a decision, a belief, or an action marks the difference between who is "in" and who is "out." Exclusivity demands that one who identifies with the Christian community stands for something, not for everything. At its best it engages and focuses energy and anchors community life.

Inclusivity goes in the other direction. It opens its arms wide to the diversity of the world, inviting the stranger into commuity without question. At its best it represents hospitality and prevenient grace—acceptance before it is asked for or earned. It points to the acceptance of the unacceptable.

At its worst it degrades the meaning of membership to a laissez faire "anything goes."

As churches seek forms for living in the coming age, the polarity of exclusivity and inclusivity will continue in tension. Because the structures of the parish tended to fall over backwards in the direction of inclusivity, local churches with an "establishment" heritage and orientation are likely to be working to discover how to fix boundaries that help members and nonmembers differentiate from one another.

These three polarities, then, are the fields of force within which the church must build new structures and processes of what it means to be the called-out people—the *ecclesia*. It is within the tension of these polarities that the church will be called on to address the formation of its laity, the new roles of the clergy, the function of oversight, and the locus of theology. It is to those issues that we turn now.

The Formation of the Laity

During the time of the Christendom Paradigm, the formation of the laity
was a matter of little concern. The entire social order was supposed to be
so rooted and grounded in the Christian faith that ordinary community
life produced a faithful people. There was no subcategory of education
that was called "Christian" education—all education was that. When
Sunday Schools were invented—almost exactly two centuries ago in
Gloucester, England—they were invented for educating working class
people, especially children, in how to read and write. They were probably more akin to today's Head Start than to what we call Sunday
School. In no way were they thought of as providing specifically religious education. The gradual transformation of those institutions into
programs for religious instruction indicates how the assumptions of the
Christendom Paradigm were disappearing. All the signs pointing to
more specifically religious education are signs that people were beginning to experience a gap; community life was not providing a religious
environment.

As the Christendom Paradigm collapsed, a widespread need for
better formation of the laity in the faith thus became increasingly clear.
Wesley's genius invented the class meeting for adult training in disciple-
ship. To this day, no better model of lay formation has been invented.
The religious education movement of the late nineteenth and early
twentieth centuries, probably the largest movement of laity in American
churches, led to Sunday Schools in almost every congregation and to
strong adult Bible study classes. Immediately after World War II, many
denominations put great resources together for national Christian education programs that had wide impact.

A wealth of efforts and programs have been mounted in the half-
century since World War II: the explosion of education programs that
followed the Baby Boom children up through public school age, the
attempts at house churches, the lay witness weekend movements and
their cousins, Cursillo, Faith at Work, Serendipity, as well as the growth
of formal retreats for laity. Even parish leadership weekends have become a standard, focusing partly on formation of lay leaders and partly
on planning parish life.

But the future church will have to be even more intentional in
formation of its laity. Living in the world's ambiguous environment and

attempting to act faithfully there, every church member is on the front line, frequently alone. The canned information about the faith produced by denominational publishing houses will not fill the bill. Lay people in an uncertain environment will be called on for independent decision and action. Memorized answers will not be enough. Every local congregation will be called on to develop processes and programs to support laity on a life-long basis.

The systems of pastoral care and nurture built into the denominations are, for the most part, splendid expressions of Christendom. They provide a liturgical framework that nurtures people through the classic life-cycle events and crises: birth = baptism; puberty = confirmation; family = marriage; illness = laying on of hands; death = burial. In each case the believing community provides the human caring for those crises; the religious ministry is controlled and administered by the pastor. Although the denominations vary in how they name those crisis-responses, the processes are similar. The pastor acts a chaplain at the event, presiding over the transition from one stage to another. The community, by definition, surrounds and supports the life of the one going through the life-change, grounding the whole of life in religious meaning.

Two things make this Christendom perspective more difficult in our time. On the one hand, life is now more complex, with many *more* key transition points than ever before. The worldview that our pastoral system reflects has no space for such profound personal changes as divorce and remarriage, yet a significant part of our congregations have experienced it. Today's lay person may make two, three, or more major professional changes during their life. The churches' responses to these life-changing events is weak. Nor do we adequately respond to the mobility of our people. And today we are much more aware of the significant developmental crises of men and women moving through life. A pastoral care system that responds to this complexity, bringing the faith fresh to those many change points, is a real need. We do not have it yet. Formation of laity in the future church needs such a system.

On the other hand, the community of faith itself—the congregation—has lost some of its capacity to be a reliable ground for initiating, educating, and nurturing each person in faith.

Several issues in the formation of laity seem inescapable:

Catechumenates: Obviously the "new Christian" needs more intensive training than has been the habit of Christendom churches. We can no longer assume that the community has engaged people in any serious contact with the tradition. Near total ignorance of the biblical story and of the faith is more and more the norm. More and more new members of the church start at ground zero. Young people and adults now come to churches with absolutely no previous experience with any religious group or tradition. An acquaintance told me with astonishment of his own daughter—brought up in a "good" family, regular attender at church and Sunday School, university graduate and recipient of a Ph.D from a first-class university—who had never heard the story of Joseph and his coat of many colors! My acquaintance was astonished. I was not. The cultural environment of our younger generations is much more distant from even the stories and illustrations of the faith than previous generations. This same acquaintance noted, "When Martin Luther King said, 'Let my people go,' almost everyone who heard him knew what he meant." "I wonder," he said, "if King could get away with it today?"

The traditional name for this initiatory training, coined to describe entry into an apostolic congregation, was catechumenate. At times such entry processes involved several years of preparation and study.

Churches are already responding to this need. The Rites for Christian Initiation of Adults (RCIA) in the Roman Catholic Church is such an attempt. Churches such as Episcopal and Lutheran who have long had some kind of confirmation preparation are beefing up their programs and reemphasizing them for adults. In some cases they are even calling them catechumenates. A remarkable program called "Education for Ministry" developed by Charles Winters and others at the University of the South has been designed as a basic course in theology available across the country, to be used in congregations anywhere.

Local congregations will need to discover the system that fits their own situation. But each needs to understand the strategic importance of training for entry into the faith. Congregations in the church of the future will have to have strong entry processes, assuming very little previous knowledge or experience of religion or Christianity. Such congregations will have to set aside the time and energy to put first class attention on this need, year after year after year.

Turning-Point Ministries: More important than the program for preparing the new member, each community of faith must rethink all of its ministries to take on the character of training for formation in ministry. Many of the members who were "cradle members" entered their churches—at whatever age they entered—pretty much as one entered Christendom. One got in by being born to a family in the congregation. Individual preparation received at the time might be adequate for one who is a back-bench supporter of mission, but it is unlikely to have been adequate for one charged with front line mission responsibility.

Life-crisis ministry for the future church will be seen as opportunities for formation of the laity. Each such moment will also be important for remedial education for those of us who come to it as Christians inadequately formed by earlier experience in the Christendom Paradigm. Each life-crisis will need to be seen as an opportunity for growing deeper in faith—not just getting through the crisis. Job-change, divorce, marriage, remarriage, retirement, going to work after retirement, breaking up from a relationship that was not a marriage, discovery that a friend or a friend's child has AIDS, going into a nursing home—each of these crises is a personal challenge. It is also an opportunity for the community of faith to help a person go deeper into faith and into a new stage of ministry. Pastoral care in an age such as we inhabit needs to be catechumenal care as well.

The adult and children's education programs of local churches need enhancement in two particulars. Because adults and children receive less of the Christian heritage from the social order, our ordinary educational programs need to concentrate on the basics and assume less. Secondly, these programs need to take very seriously a study of the social environment as a field of mission. For adults and children alike we need to develop "mission training" to help each person to cross the mission frontier more responsibly. Case studies, story-telling, and community analysis need to become staples of religious engagement for church members. I would love to see congregations develop programs of "field work" in mission—sending members out Monday through Friday conscious of being on a mission and using class time on the weekend to reflect and report or to share cases of mission they had attempted during the week.

Every congregation also has a major opportunity in this mobile society to provide membership training for everyone who moves to town and seeks to join. Regardless of the newcomer's former involvement or noninvolvement in church, *every* time she or he enters a new faith-community is an invaluable time when training should be mandated.

In the time of Christendom, infants were assumed to be born into and nurtured by a parish that was a community of faith. Baptism of infants made sense in many different denominations, including my own. In this age, when we cannot assume that a child will be nurtured within a faith community, we simply have to rethink what the churches mean by baptism and how they structure their life to bring the young to faithful maturity. This rethinking involves deeply loved practices and long-held theological positions. It requires something more than tinkering with the age of baptism and admission to communion. It requires more than a Saturday afternoon hour with lovely pagan godparents! The problem is acute right now for those who practice infant baptism, but it is no less important for those whose practice is different.

The Reformation of the Clergy

Clergy are a critical part of our problem. Many of them are uncomfortably aware of that fact, but believe someone else is responsible for their pain. During a thousand years of Christendom the churches built a power system controlled by the clergy—a clericalism that now distorts power relationships. In the beginning I am sure that was not the intent; the intent was to use talented people to strengthen the church's life. The call for ordained leaders to shape and guide the institution was needed and was remarkably effective.

The power system that nevertheless developed continues to be in place, but it has less and less to do with the church's sense of its mission. A layman once told me how it feels to him: "I didn't know the church existed as an employment system for clergy."

In the Church of Christendom, the clergy were assumed to play the primary role in mission and ministry. In the emerging church, the laity are the primary ones to cross the missionary frontier and undertake the missionary task. Many clergy feel displaced and have difficulty accepting the new lay authority. What is more, they do not have a sense of what new role they should bear.

Thus, no one faces a greater change in the future church than clergy. In the past four decades they have already experienced more change than they expected. From being a high-status/low-stress profession the clergy has become a low-status/high-stress profession. The number of congregations who can afford to pay their pastor a living wage has declined.

In the next generation we must produce clergy who can support the ministry of others and train them, rather than act out of a need to control their ministries. Clergy leadership must be unabashedly religious and spiritual, but they will also have to be flexible and creative managers of institutional structures, coping with all kinds of changes. They will have to become imaginative stewards, frequently operating with decreasing resources. They must be single-minded in commitment to building up and equipping the people of God for their new mission in the new age.

Clergy are, I believe, a key resource for the future church. They are badly needed to ground the new structures in which lay people will gather to be formed and sent. They are critical training officers for the church of the future. The educational systems we have for training clergy, however, were invented to produce pastoral leadership for a Christendom Church. Those systems know how to add or change course offerings, but they still—as educational systems—prepare for a role and a world that parish pastors no longer face. Seminaries face the need for major changes while facing escalating costs and decreased resources.

It may be more important that we develop the tools, resources, or energy constantly to retrain clergy *after* seminary. I emphasize *constantly*. We seem to be able to gather the energy for any kind of exciting experiment or program even when resources are scarce. But what is needed is long-distance attention, the ability to establish and continue to support training year after year as successive classes move out from theological education, using their experience as the curriculum for re-training.

The Shape of Church Oversight (*Episcopé*)

The structures for providing oversight of the churches have long been a cause of infighting in denominations. Rethinking the location of the mission frontier forces us to rethink the functions of oversight. That will require each denomination to rethink the structures so they will serve the functions more adequately. Here the issues are not about what you *call* them, bishops or presbyteries or conferences or conventions or superintendents; I am talking about what those people or groups *do*.

In the Christendom Paradigm, that function was mostly exercised by talented professional staffs and bishops who administered programs or processes larger than of those at the congregational level and that linked the local congregation to far-off concerns of mission.

If I am right, every congregation will face major stress in the coming decades. More, not less. Power will shift. Financial systems will be affected. Relations with congregations will change. Basic frameworks may have to be redesigned. The old model of oversight will not be adequate. In many places even today it is in crisis or collapse already.

Episcopé, the function of oversight, is the sum total of how each denomination makes available all the help they can give to those on the local scene. Congregations of the next few decades face needs that are greater than ever, and their need for help from their system of *episcopé* will far outstrip the capacity of the systems.

As the clergy face daunting tasks of retooling for a very different kind of ministry than most of them thought they had bought into, even more so will those providing oversight be challenged to change and adapt. Just keeping up with pastoral care for clergy overwrought by stress will be overwhelming. Beyond that is the larger task of retraining the clergy and providing a steady, dependable institutional framework.

One particular point makes the new role of oversight difficult. In the age of the Christendom Paradigm, the flow of resources was from the congregation through the regional structure to the far-off mission frontier. As we think about organizations, that was a flow "up" from the local situation to the "higher" office and then to the frontier. That set relationships in one direction. In the age of the future church, with the mission frontier close to the local congregation, the flow of resources and attention needs to be reversed. Those in oversight need to shift emotional and functional relations with congregations by 180 degrees. If resources are to flow to the mission frontier, they must be flowing primarily toward the local congregation, not away from it. That is an enormous change.

Here I worry about several things: the increasingly severe financial constraints at the regional and national levels of the denominations, the almost total lack of training and retraining models for these key persons, and the almost total lack of support systems for them. There is virtually no research on this critical leadership function in the churches.

In all the denominations, by whatever names we call it, we badly need a better functioning system by which local churches, clergy, and laity are strengthened and encouraged into their ministries. The old system of oversight approaches collapse.

Theology in the Future Church

In the age of Christendom, the work of theology became more and more
an enterprise of the academy and its professionals and less and less rele-
vant to everyday life. The theological frontier was addressed in learned
study and in the library, but the ordinary Christian had little knowledge
of its usefulness. As a matter of fact, even among professional theologians usefulness was not often a high-level objective. A decade ago, a
colleague had occasion to do a study of decision making at a group of
theological seminaries concerned about their future. He discovered that
in no case in his sample did anybody in those seminaries make reference
to a theological idea or principle in the decisions that were being made.
The same thing can obviously be said of theology's relationship to most
parish debates and decisions, most family decisions, or the decisions we
make about our work. Theology has become a classroom exercise just
when we need most to have it available to guide us on the new mission
frontier.

In the new *ecclesia* the primary theologians have to be the laity
because they are on the missionary frontier. They will need to be theologians for two reasons: First, because as our primary mission officers
they will be engaging the world, making judgements, and seeking God's
direction. Second, because it is on that frontier that God will be reveal-
ing God's nature, opening doors to the new theologies of tomorrow's
world. The laity will be on the front lines of theology as well as mission.

Clergy and theological faculties need to be retooled to become resource persons *to* lay theologians. I have sometimes characterized the
current system as a "trickle down" system of theology: We try to get
extremely good theologians to teach in seminaries, hoping they in turn
will somehow get "enough" theology into their students that they will
somehow preach and teach "enough" into the lives of the laity so they
can get by. To say it is to recognize its absurdity. Yet, there is something in our system that operates that way.

Clergy and theological faculties are not trained to do it backwards,
as I am suggesting they must. If the laity are to become the functioning
theologians on the mission frontier, they will badly need well-trained,
deeply-grounded specialists who know not just the historical tradition,
but how to ask questions and probe today's experience. I have seen
models for this in the training being given to mentors in the Education

for Ministry course—lay people and clergy being taught to help laity reflect theologically on cases of their own experiences in work and community life. There are gifted educators using supervisory skills to help laity elicit learning from experience. Some cell groups put a high value on exploring experience theologically.

In our present system most of our theological training for laity frankly looks like watered-down seminary classes. Gregory Baum, the Canadian theologian, once described it to me as a kind of "Super Sunday School." The curriculum, the methods of teaching follow seminary models, but the work is less demanding. Perhaps we should not be surprised that the net effect, often, is that we simply underline the thing we hope to avoid. We reinforce the old idea that the only "real" ministry is ordained ministry. The people going through the lay training systems get that deeper message and more and more present themselves for formal theological training. The last state is worse than the first.

The development of this new kind of theology really depends on partnership between clergy and laity. We need clergy and theologians to mine the Scriptures and the theological traditions and discover new ways to use those resources in listening and questioning the laity about the mission frontier. We need the laity to take authority as the church's operating theologians, acting on the frontier with confidence in the power of the Spirit, but also searching and reflecting to discern God's purposes. I believe this requires a new kind of partnership in learning between clergy and laity.

The future church demands a new locus of theology, a change from the library and university to the place where the baptized person encounters the world, the place I have called the missionary frontier. The future church demands a new actor in the work of theology: the baptized lay person. The future church demands a new kind of training center for theology: the local church.

What the seminary has been for ministry in the nineteenth and twentieth centuries, the local congregation must be in the twenty-first.

If this really happens, theology as an enterprise will be vastly changed. Many clergy and theologians will feel this as a loss of their power and their special role. They may feel very threatened, unless they understand that power expands as it is shared.

The Church Upside Down

I am describing a church turned on its head. Upside down. At least it seems so. Although roles, relationships, and centers of organization and power seem to be turned around, the orientation to the mission frontier is the same. It is just that the frontier has moved from the far-off edge of Empire to the doors of the local congregation.

I have a friend who once asked me over to watch the Super Bowl. We sat in his den, my wife and I, he and his wife. At the half time his four teenage children roared in with Cokes and pretzels and six friends. We could no longer fit into the den. We had to move the TV to the living room, shift all the furniture around, and reorganize ourselves to see the second half. We had to change nearly everything to go on doing what we had already been doing and wanted to continue.

The church is always focused on its mission. In the Christendom Paradigm it understood that mission one way and organized its life to accomplish it. We have awakened to find out that the mission moved on us. To keep focusing on mission, we have to turn the furniture around and face a different direction. We may have to move into another room. For many of us, it is going to feel very different, as if the world were turned upside down, but the function and direction of our calling demands that we turn around.

The Church of Christendom structured itself to address mission beyond the Empire. That meant that it built parish systems, regional structures, and national entities that could gather and deploy resources to the critical point on the missionary frontier. Because that frontier was far away, it required the kinds of logistics and organization it takes to mount a military campaign in a far-off land. There were lots of training camps to prepare the key troops, special training for the leaders, airplanes and ships for transport, policy decisions at high levels at meetings of the generals and the prime ministers, and total support from the citizens at home.

That's the church we built. It served well—for that understanding of mission.

But the missionary frontier has changed. It's gone local. In the above analogy, it is as if the far-off battle ended and a new one emerged on the home front—let's say an epidemic of drug use and addiction. Our impulse would be to attack *that* crisis in the way that worked before. We would announce a War on Drugs and appoint a national czar. We would develop great strategies and even train new armies. We might call out the army and the National Guard. We would try to develop more sophisticated weapons.

The example makes the obvious point. The same approach does not work if the problem is that different. The misuse of drugs is predominately a local problem, involving decisions of individuals, the life of families and neighborhoods, and schools and playgrounds. Bombs, even *smart* bombs, won't work. We can't even use them on the parts of the problem that *are* larger than local.

That's what's happened to the church.

The structures designed for one mission do not work in the new mission. The church upside down has not changed at its heart. Its focus is still mission, but the mission location has changed.

A system designed to deliver resources far away must redesign itself to address a missionary frontier at home, one that literally surrounds the local congregation. The national and regional structures designed to send resources far away must change to face the thousands of local situations where the mission frontier touches each congregation.

The leaders in this mission are the laity. The first-line resource people and trainers are also laity—experienced, theologically solid laity. The laity are supported by the clergy.

The clergy and the laity are the strategic teams, but they have to learn a new way to work together. The regional structures—bishops, executives, conferences, presbyteries—are the strategic reserves. They must have the tools and the flexibility to get resources to the congregations in the thick of the mission when there are challenges, opportunities, or breakdowns. The region may also be able to see farther down the pike and be aware of dimensions of challenge that local people have not noticed. The national structures become the second line of reserves, focused on training systems and research.

Impediments to Change

I have tried to be honest about the significant resistance I see to the changes that lie ahead in building the church of the future. Now I want to address several specific areas in which we must be prepared to work with or around impediments. I see them as of two types: structural and personal.

Structural resistances refer to characteristics built into our systems by the successes of the Christendom Paradigm: strong, conservative institutional frameworks, leadership patterns, dependency-affirming relationships, and financial systems.

The institutional frameworks we have inherited from the Church of Christendom were built over centuries to provide stability and predictability. Systems of church order had those values built into their warp and woof. The primary value was the ability to hold settled communities steady on a distant unchanging goal. Flexibility was discouraged and uniformity encouraged. Books of order of the different denominations reflect this bias. Such systems work where the environment is stable and the need for inventing new responses is low. Such systems affirm fixed patterns of congregational life and discourage efforts to do things that are off the norm. In many areas of church life, these patterns continue to have high value. But in the places where new life emerges and new challenges to ministry are developing, the books of order make it difficult to be adaptive. Attention needs to be given now to opening up, even in the books of order, space for zones of experimentation where for a time the official rules may be suspended to allow something very different to be tried.

We have laity and clergy who are ready and willing to make such pioneering efforts. From past experience, I expect many of them to fail, but at times of paradigm shift like ours, we need to encourage the scouts to search out territory that lies ahead. Some will succeed. Our systems of order need to encourage their ventures, but not many do.

Inadequate leadership is also an obstacle. I make no criticism of the people in leadership roles in the denominations. I fault the denominations for the system of leadership that sets impossible tasks without adequate support and training, and without clear delegation of authority. Our leaders reflect the inadequacies of our systems. But there are several areas of specific inadequacy.

We and our leaders have a poor theology of institutions. We do not see the very structure of institutions as possible servants of God and gifts for ministry. In consequence, we look at our institutions as albatrosses hanging about our necks and dragging us down. I contend that institutions and specifically the church as it is, warts and all, is one of God's most graceful gifts to God's people. Without a biblical theology of the spiritual power of the corporate, modern church people are at the mercy of a shallow individualism that is cultural and not scriptural. Indeed, without such an understanding and without the spiritual power of the community of the church, we are helpless to deal with the substantial and ambiguous corporate powers of which St. Paul warned us. Without such a theology and commitment on the part of its leaders, the church has little power to address the profound issues of change that it faces.

There are specific areas in which this poor theology penalizes the church that attempts to work for the future. The unwillingness of clergy as a group to face their profound ambivalence about money acts as a barrier to their own financial stewardship and that of the church's people. The common wisdom passed about among the clergy that parish endowments are the creature of the devil is a case in point. That "wisdom" is profoundly unscriptural and gets in the way of the desire of many church people to contribute financially to the future church.

But the issue of inadequacy of leadership is far larger than ambivalence about money. The inadequacy of the leadership reflects the inadequacy of the membership. The invasion of the church by cultural values about money and its relation to success and effectiveness is the broader frame of reference needed to work out what has happened—the erosion of the church's clarity about what it is vis-a-vis the environment.

The dependency system fostered by the Church of Christendom remains a barrier to building a church for the future. The hierarchical arrangement that grew in the institution through its life was a response to the worldview of its leaders. It was reinforced by the leaders' interpretations of history, and it facilitated responding to the missionary frontier at the edge of the Empire. These reinforcing systems contain unhealthy structures. In an earlier generation we described this as a classically Parent-Child institutional arrangement, locking the child into permanent dependence. In today's language of Twelve Step Programs we describe this as a co-dependent system. Whatever the language or image, we are pointing to the fact that the church has a culture that encourages some to take responsibility for the lives and behavior of others, with loss of authority and independence to those others. Systems that continue as Parent-Child or co-dependent systems will block the development of the kind of individual responsibility and authority that only can shape a church responsive to the new mission frontier.

Personal resistances to change exist within everyone. I see them within the framework of the behaviors Elizabeth Kubler-Ross used to describe another kind of grief. Indeed, facing the changes of leaving one age of the church and discovering another may be most analagous to a kind of death. Following Kubler-Ross, then:

Denial is the behavior I see used most often as a barrier. I see denial in congregations continuing to operate as if nothing has changed. Churches or congregations in denial look at downward patterns of membership and finance and talk about how it seems to be "bottoming out." Denial can be seen in the congregation that gradually eats up its reserves in deficit budgets year after year, with no thought to what comes next. Denial is a good word to describe congregations who put off capital needs for future generations to face. Denial exists in denominations using scare tactics and crisis methods to generate temporary support for continuing on a collision course with disaster.

Denial also exists where clergy and executives put their heads down and slog ahead, doing the same thing, sometimes a little bit harder. Denial is what prompts two or three congregations (or seminaries or agencies) to merge, refusing to deal with the very difficult dynamics involved, with a simple faith that something will intervene to make it work. There is a lot of denial around. So long as it is around, it will be difficult to generate energy to face needed change.

Depression is almost equally present in congregations and judicatories. Depleted energy, listlessness, and a lack of imagination or leadership sucks people into a slow downward spiral. In depression there is often a sense of the depth of the disease but no capacity to respond. Depressed congregations may quietly hope for a miracle, but they do not expect it. Depressed clergy and executives doggedly hang on by their fingernails, trying to make it to retirement. They no longer expect to make any difference.

Bargaining is the arena of the "the new program will fix it" people. Sensing the loss of the familiar, such people latch onto some new action they can take that will turn back the clocks to the golden age. A new program of evangelism, a new hymnal, a new bishop or denominational president, a new prophetic issue solved—all are potential options for the bargaining response to the loss of certainty.

Anger is the most visible response. Much of the bitter anger in the theological and political conflicts in our denominations comes from the depths of persons who have a sense of loss of the church they loved. The conflicts may be about substantial concerns, but often the anger that surrounds them comes from those feelings of loss. I see this anger in bitter debates leading to the firing of some pastors. I see it in the way clergy scapegoat their executives or denomination. I see it in the way clergy talk about their lay people and the way lay people talk about clergy. I see it in the way people at all levels engage in civil wars or try to purge one another for one reason or another. I do not deny the fact that there is often truth behind many of the angers, but our age of change and the loss of the familiar puts a bitter edge to the anger, often violating the spirit of community. Building a church for the future will take all the sense of community we can get.

But if we are to move beyond these barriers, we must move in the direction of the dying patient toward the one stance that can truly deal with the monumental change from the old order of death to the new order of acceptance. The era of Christendom is over. Change is our future. How do we bring it about?

Resources for Change

When we look at the need for major changes throughout the religious systems—indeed, the reinvention of the churches—we can be overwhelmed, but there are substantial resources available. Let me name and describe some of the most obvious:

Theological seminaries. Nearly 200 accredited theological seminaries are spread over the face of the land. Of course they vary enormously in strength as institutions and in their financial and human resources. Some are barely surviving. Others are strong with imaginative leadership. Some have two or three score students, some number their matriculants in the thousands. Each seminary is a pool of talented thinkers and scholars, and each has made significant contributions to religious leadership.

We sometimes forget that theological seminaries themselves are testimony to the adaptive capacity of American churches. Less than 200 years ago, faced with the expanding need for clergy to lead congregations in the new nation, American church leaders invented seminaries. Those seminaries met the need, and they still produce well-schooled pastors, scholars, and denominational leaders. The seminaries exemplify the inventiveness of American churches.

If we become overwhelmed by the problems of reinventing church structures, we can take considerable comfort in how American churches have already demonstrated remarkable adaptability in their invention of a national system of theological education, generating really massive resources to make it happen.

What is disturbingly clear, however, is the difficulty seminaries are having in adapting to the changed conditions of church life as the twenty-first century approaches. The costs of the theological education escalate geometrically. As inflation has led to shrinking endowments, more and more of the costs of theological education are being carried by student tuition.

Churches are called to supply more and more financial resources for candidates who provide significantly less service as professional leaders. The typical seminary graduate of 1950 could be expected to serve forty years before retirement; a typical graduate of 1990 will serve only twenty-five to thirty years or less—meaning that the cost of educating clergy *per year of service to the church* is twenty-five to fifty percent higher in *hidden* costs over the past half-century, to say nothing of the escalation of the visible costs in budgets.

The ability of the churches to sustain that model of education in the face of dwindling "job openings" is questionable. A letter from Princeton Seminary to Presbyterian leaders in 1991, for example, noted 152 entry-level job openings for which there were a total of 1,500 applicants; the Episcopal Church reports that in 1955 the number of total available seminary graduates to open positions was in a ratio of 1/1; in 1990 it was two graduates per job.

Several seminaries, however, suggest that imagination can redirect seminary resources into new forms of service to the church of the future:

> In 1939, a small Presbyterian seminary in upstate New York faced a dwindling need for its traditional services. Instead of accepting a long, slow demise, the trustees took a bold step. They sold the property and moved, lock, stock, and barrel to New York City. There they kept their name, formed a partnership with Union Seminary, and started a new life. There Auburn Seminary developed new services for its constituency, becoming a center of continuing education and a support system for Presbyterians at Union Seminary. Even as this is being written, Auburn, led by Barbara Wheeler, is expanding its role by developing a center for research in theological education.

Hartford Seminary (United Church of Christ) faced similar dynamics and a reduced pool of students in the 1960s. Under the leadership of a courageous board and president, Hartford transformed itself from a "standard" seminary into an institution that focuses on research and continuing education. The move was painful for many and required major changes. Hartford has become, however, a significant resource for those attempting to build a new church. Its research has broken new ground for religious life, especially for the mainline denominations.

A number of seminaries run by Catholic orders in the Washington, D.C., area, shattered by drops in vocations to holy orders, chose to band together in a Theological Coalition under Dr. Vincent Cushing. Instead of several marginal and dying institutions, they have fashioned a living coalition.

There is clearly a limited pool of funds with which to fund theological seminaries. The dramatic increase in the cost of seminary education per year of professional service rendered already is forcing the churches to reexamine their investment.

Yet, as the Auburn, Hartford, and Washington examples show, theological seminaries can be remarkable clusters of imagination, leadership, and financial resources. Where they can find a vision of new contributions to the emerging church, they may successfully address options for the future.

One worries, however, that the pain of change and the inertia of old ways will trap too many seminaries in continued, downward spirals. Tenure systems alone make it difficult to change directions with any speed. It takes strength, courage, and resources to change. Those who wait too long may use up the resources and have no energy left for even essential changes.

Our current structures. From local church to national denominational board our religious organizations and structures and the people in them represent enormous resources, energy, and experience. I do find mindless bureaucrats in some church offices, but they are the exception. On the whole I find imagination and commitment when I meet executives or program directors and their staffs. When they are frustrated—and many of them are—it is usually because they see how unproductive

some of the patterns and programs with which they work are. One fact
that most of them live with is that they have been experiencing declining
real income for two to three decades while local congregations and
clergy have not reduced their expectations. They are expected to operate
fully in the model of Christendom while at the same time helping congregations and regional structures realign themselves to the new mission
frontier.

One great strength these systems bring is the flow of financial
resources–by far the greatest philanthropic phenomenon in our society.
This flow is supported by the dedicated stewardship of ordinary church
members, but it has been developed, organized, and stimulated by careful
denominational efforts over the generations. This flow has funded the
extraordinary set of buildings and institutions through which churches do
their work—from modest rented store fronts to majestic cathedrals and
modern office buildings.

There are offsetting and severe problems in the financial area. In
many places, funding increases no longer keep pace with inflation.
Local congregations face a squeeze, regional institutions face a crunch,
and national agencies face near catastrophe as people first fund the religious structures that deal most closely with their perceptions of need,
with their understanding of where mission lies.

Crises multiply. Maintenance on great buildings is deferred. In
many places the buildings are far more expensive than their current
members can sustain. Increases in medical insurance and utility costs
play havoc with budgets. Current needs outrun the availability of current
funds.

The problem is really a double-bind. The church is torn by well-
deserved guilt when its budgets simply support a comfortable, self-
concerned congregation. But both economic shortfall and the concern
for "outreach" make the church neglect its infrastructure, allowing its
institutions to erode and lose their vitality. Churches—local, regional, or
national—invest nothing in research and development. This is a serious
lack. One must note, however, the critically important role played by
several foundations, most notably the Lilly Endowment of Indianapolis.
Established by a caring and devoted Episcopal businessman, this founda-
tion supports more research on religious life, as far as I can tell, than all
the denominations put together!

The need is urgent for two things: more *imagination* in helping every congregation, judicatory, and board begin radically restructuring its life and *significant new resources,* certainly the development of resources that can support experimentation and study, trial efforts, and skilled advisory services to those attempting change.

Changing church structures in any significant way takes time, energy, imagination, *and* money. Change takes *more* than is needed to maintain the steady, slowly declining state. If significant time, energy, imagination, and money are not allocated for change, the future is clear; gradual depletion of resources, using up of assets, and dissipation of energy. There are already too many national systems, theological seminaries, regional judicatories, and congregations where that downward spiral has become irreversible.

The people themselves. People of good will and deep commitment fill our churches today. They are there because they believe in what the church proclaims. They are there because they want to be there. They are there to give themselves to a cause larger than themselves. They are there to be fed and to grow.

One cannot say enough good about this asset.

Over recent generations the giving of committed people to their churches has increased substantially. Actual declines in giving to religious institutions come from decreased numbers in the pews; the evidence is that those who remain behind are more and more generous with their giving. They give money and time, although life-style changes (particularly the increased number of women in the labor force) have made a difference in how they can give time. The demographics of this group have changed, too, with increased age a part of the picture in mainline denominations.

A new breed of change agents. The church is generating a new asset base in the band of change-agents, entrepreneurial organizations, and talented consultants who can provide back-up resources for those who *want* to change. There are many kinds speaking languages of change. Stephen Ministries works with congregations to develop lay pastoral ministries. Paul Dietterich and his colleagues at Chicago's Center for Parish Development bring revitalization skills to pastors, lay leaders, and executives. The Institute for Church Growth in California does research, teaching, and consulting focused on helping congregations expand their membership in size and depth. Lyle Schaller exemplifies the peripatetic consultant across the country, meanwhile turning out an unprecedented flow of books and articles to help those engaged in leadership. There are several score of similar itinerant consultants, none of whom approaches Schaller in written production. Herbert Miller and the National Association of Evangelicals provide resources and expertise.

The Congregational Studies Task Group, an informal gathering of religious leaders, teachers, and researchers, has now spent a decade developing resources and books to support change in religious life at the level of the local church. Their best-known and most widely-used resource is the *Handbook for Congregational Studies,* published by Abingdon in 1989.

The Alban Institute provides research, education, publishing, and consulting across the continent from its home office in Washington, D.C., and through its national network of consultants.

There are more. One characteristic of this time of change seems to be the proliferation of resource people.

These people and agencies exist because people facing change in their religious systems need help. They seem, more and more, to be eager to get help wherever they can get it, whether it comes from within their denomination or not. The rapid growth of these groups in the last two decades is testimony to how serious church leaders are about rebuilding the structures they have inherited. These groups also model how the role and function of *episcopé* may emerge in the next generation or two.

Anybody who wants to begin rebuilding toward what God is calling the church to be can find help.

Summary

We are at the front edges of the greatest transformation of the church that has occurred for 1,600 years. It is by far the greatest change that the church has ever experienced in America; it may eventually make the transformation of the Reformation look like a ripple in a pond.

That transformation is occurring because of the persistent call of God that our whole world be made new, and that the church's mission in that world be itself transformed in new patterns of reconciling the world to God.

There are enormous tasks and daunting challenges for those who intend to follow that call, but then the Lord never said it would be easy.

CHAPTER V

Principles and Strategies for Building the Future Church and Some Signs of Its Presence

Principles and Strategies

Because we cannot know the exact shape of the future, it is all the more important to identify principles to hold onto as we work toward it. If one cannot see the land, it is all the more important to understand how to use maps and compasses and to know the currents of the sea and how the wind blows. Today, as never before, we are aware that the future is blowing in the wind.

The new discipline of congregational studies describes four dimensions of congregational life that need to be probed by those who would understand or change congregations:

— *program* is the sum total of the things a congregation does, including what is on its calendar;

— *process* is the way the congregation does what it does: how its leadership works, how its people and groups make choices and relate to one another;

— *context* is the setting in the community and the denomination, the external forces that constrain or influence what the congregation and its members are and do; and

— *identity* is that rich mix of memory and meaning that grounds the congregation, defining who it really is in its heart.

Most of the attempts I see to change congregational life in response to the dislocations I have described seem to be in the area of tinkering with program. Denominations develop new program emphases, regional judicatories announce "this year's crusade," which usually coincides with the annual pledge campaign. Nobody expects much to change. There is a conspiracy of silence, hoping that things will be no worse next year than last. In places where rapid growth is occurring, there is increasing pressure to strengthen and broaden program offerings and staff for new needs. When growth is not happening, the pressure approaches desperation. The assumption seems to be that the answer is to get the best program ideas and put them to work.

The attention paid to context is primarily to find out how to market the program already adopted or how to adapt the program to be a better fit with the population in the area of the local congregation. At its best, this tinkering produces better program, better connected to its potential audience. At its worst, it falls captive to the kind of marketing that simply repackages old goods and flogs them to a new audience.

If we are, as I am convinced, in a time in which the paradigms are changing, a cosmetic approach to change, the kind that deals with surface appearances, is inadequate. Organizational specialists distinguish between "transitional" and "transformational" change. By transitional change they mean the adaptations and shifts brought on by temporary dislocations and discomforts, moving to a new stability. By transformational change they mean the shattering of the foundations and the reconstitution of a new entity.

Churches that tinker with program and marketing are barely beginning to be on the edge of transitional change, but the building of the future church requires transformation at its very core. We are not looking for cosmetic changes or the kind of "fixes" that come in annual program cycles; we are looking for several generations of struggle with our identity as people of God, with how we live together, with what our environment really is. As we do that struggling we will have to generate program, revise our structures, and adopt new roles.

To mount that struggle with identity, process, and context, however, requires that we start where we are in the church we have, caught as it is in the time between paradigms. As we do, there are some principles and strategies that we can hold onto. It may be that none of these principles and strategies is new or unique, but they are the distillation of experience accumulated from two decades of listening to and working with people in several hundred congregations, several scores of judicatories in several dozen denominations.

Looking for learning points

Change in an evolutionary time does not occur everywhere at the same rate. Most organizational structures, as well as our own expectations, assume that it is the same everywhere. Our denominations develop approaches intended to fit every situation and every congregation as if they were the same, and as if they all lived by the same schedule. That approach often produces answers that therefore fit nowhere.

At The Alban Institute we have pioneered a strategy that seems to work. We look for what we call "learning points," those moments special to a single congregation when those particular people feel a challenge to change and are ready to act. These points are unique. Sometimes they do not last long.

We find that effort to work toward these learning points doubles and redoubles the effectiveness of the change effort.

Some learning points are cyclical and almost predictable, like the change of pastors. Others are quite unpredictable, like the unexpected collapse of an institution or a person, or even a building. Almost any kind of crisis within the system can be a learning point. We find that the break-out of a severe fight or a major economic change in the community can precipitate such an opportunity.

Whether these learning points—predictable or unpredictable—lead to change or not depends on a number of things. If the people in the situation are overwhelmed by the moment, if they are unwilling to accept the opportunity within the challenge, or if the outside resources are not responsive and available, the moment may pass with nothing to show but a papered-over crack in the wall. Similarly, if the people are burned out emotionally or have used up all their resources, they cannot rise to the occasion and use the learning point as a moment for change. The opportunity will pass and may not recur for some years.

Moments like this are scary and threatening to the people who lead congregations. They bring out all kinds of defensiveness ("Nobody can tell us what to do"), anger ("If so-and-so hadn't messed up, we wouldn't be in this boat"), depression ("I give up"), and a host of less palatable behaviors.

Moments like this call for strong outside support. This is the opportunity for imaginative oversight by whoever has the call to the function —whether bishop or executive, judicatory staff person, lay leader from the next parish, or consultant. If consultants are called in, they frequently ask the question of oversight in a proposal—"I think the problem is this, and I suggest these three steps to deal with it. It will cost this much. Do you want to work on it?" For the congregation that may be the moment of truth. Some congregations take up the moment. I know many who say "No" to the consultant, but nevertheless act on the problem. Others say "Yes," but do not make a real commitment. But that moment is an open opportunity.

I have also seen judicatory staff exercise oversight at such moments ("I'll send you our guidelines for dealing with that, but how about letting me come out to talk to the group to help you figure out what to do?"). I have known a lay leader from another congregation to be the one exercising the function ("That is a mess. We ran into it last year before our annual meeting. Let me tell you how we dealt with it and where we got help.")

I think the most important function of the judicatory is to provide that kind of oversight. It requires careful and continuing listening to congregations and their lay and clergy leadership. It means interpreting attacks, not getting defensive. It means reading the bulletins and listening to the scuttlebutt at meetings, being prepared to step in when a learning moment seems to have arrived. It means hearing the issues behind the griping and complaining. It also means working to increase the kinds of resources that are appropriate to different learning points. No judicatory in these days can afford to have a staff that is prepared to respond to all kinds of crises. The best judicatories, in my opinion, operate primarily in intervention, providing a wide menu of trusted resources with which the congregation can address its issue. A judicatory that does this well will discover that there is no need to mount independent judicatory programming efforts.

There are political implications to working strategically as I suggest here. Expectations that judicatories have of themselves, and that many congregations have of their judicatories, are that program is equally accessible to all. If you take seriously the importance of learning points, you know that those expectations are wrong.

The alternative to the focused use of resources on congregations that are at change-points is a wasteful scattering of resources. Bureaucracies tend to try to make everything available to everybody, with the result that no one's needs are met. Denominational offices have to think and act strategically in their use of resources in a way that focuses those resources on the individual.

Let me address the judicatory with my naked point: "Put all your energy into congregations that are at learning points. The others? *Leave them alone!"*

Working experimentally

Under the Christendom Paradigm, churches have structured themselves for uniformity and permanence. Congregations in one place think they need to be like congregations in other places in style, program, and behavior. They and their program need to be relatively unchanging. Nothing gets started that is not intended to become permanent.

Thinking that way helped when their mission was primarily to produce resources for the far-off mission frontier. That mission did not change much over the years, and the prime need was for steadiness and predictability in responding to that mission.

But in a time of change, when pressure and opportunity for change are not the same everywhere, we badly need innovators, people and groups who will take a stab at a new way with the freedom to fail.

The structures of the church, formed as they were for stability and endurance, mitigate against innovation. How many experiments in the churches have worn themselves out trying to get permission from the legal entities of the denominations? Where the experiment did get off to a limping start, often the suspicious requirements for reporting and justifying the change wore down the innovative enthusiasm. Of course, when that happens, the system says, "There! We knew it wouldn't last!".

The churches must learn to encourage innovation and even fund it, rather than handicap and punish it. We must encourage innovation to find some new paths and to get models of innovation widely known. Eventually every congregation will need the capacity to approach its uniqueness with innovative energy. Meanwhile, in times and places where change is rapid, our most important asset is the pioneer, the one—or the many—who is willing to break new paths. We need to honor them, even when they fail, recognizing that even though some may fail, we can still learn from the attempt.

I am aware of two ways in which we undercut the effectiveness of experimentation. In the first case we do not make a commitment that is sufficiently long. Change in religious institutions takes time. I remember one presbytery that authorized and funded an exciting new effort to start a congregation. In only six months the leadership of the congregation discovered that they had to start defending what they were doing on the presbytery floor. The presbytery really had made inadequate commitment to experimentation. They counted on fast results in an area in which fast results are not possible. They were unwilling to give the experiment enough time. Experiments do not work if you keep pulling them up to look at the roots.

Denominations and congregations also undercut experimentation by excessive turnover of leadership. Many small church projects that are started with real enthusiasm by one group of judicatory staff and leaders founder when a new group of leaders comes in or a key staff person changes. Two areas in the Episcopal Church with outstanding experimental support for small congregations—the Diocese of Nevada and a deanery of the Diocese of New York around Upper Boiceville—owe much of their success to continuity of leadership. Two bishops in succession saw the strategy the same way, and one archdeacon has stayed put for two decades. It is not easy to find one judicatory leader who is willing to support the basic strategies of her or his predecessor. It is even more rare to find a staff person who stays in place long enough to give a framework of policy stability.

Even more painful to me is the way we negate experiments by neglecting to capture and communicate what is learned. The church all too often walks away from pieces of its work with no effort to share its successes and failures. This is enormously wasteful. There are file cabinets in the basement of every judicatory and every national denomination full of information about important attempts to solve problems or install change. Nobody opens the files or even remembers who did it. Those of us who have been around for a while often run into projects that are being announced as "the first ever," and we remember others who worked hard on the same issue perhaps a decade ago. The new pioneer is often unaware of the trails others blazed in earlier generations.

Working experimentally is a key to making some of the changes we need to make for the future church.

Paying attention to boundaries

In 1976, The Alban Institute was attracted to a concept that has become foundational for us in understanding and searching for the meanings of change. The concept was the "boundary." We believe the concept has broad usefulness for those seeking to build the future church.

The concept of the boundary came to us as we studied what happened when a seminary student moved from the seminary into her or his first assignment. We wanted to find out why the dedicated efforts of seminaries across the country to help their graduates become better prepared for ministry in congregations all had the same result—graduates, with varying degrees of anger, saying "Why didn't the seminary prepare me for this?"

We discovered that the problem was not a lack of information or anything of that sort. Nor was it a lack of imagination or effort on the part of seminaries. It was a matter of two cultures, seminary culture and congregational culture. They were different, including different ways of thinking and working, different reward systems and values, even different languages. Our study (some results of which were published in Roy Oswald's Alban monograph, *Crossing the Boundary*, [1] and in Harbaugh, *et al., Beyond the Boundary*[2]) focused on the extraordinary experience people had when they moved from one institution to another. It was frightening and invigorating; it was also a moment of potentially extraordinary growth and learning. We decided that boundaries were worth watching as important definers of change.

We found many other boundaries, each one of which has unusual potential for growth—in emotional and spiritual depth, and in relationships. Each also provided an unmatched opportunity for learning new skills and abilities. Some of the boundaries we have since worked with others to explore are these:

- the boundary one crosses in choosing to go to church;
- the boundary a pastor crosses in moving from one congregation to another;
- the boundary a person crosses in moving from one town to another, one job to another;
- the boundary between work life and retirement;
- the boundary shaped by angry leave-taking or firing;

— the boundary from a congregation into a seminary;
— the boundary from one stage of life to the next;
— the boundary of death.

The important point for us has been the use of boundary as a metaphor for a learning opportunity. We clearly find such boundaries have very high learning potential, but in most cases the persons involved are so busy they do not stop to learn. Indeed, their very busyness is the escape mechanism most people use to avoid the pain of learning and change.

Let me give an example. The Alban Institute did a lot of research on the process by which people enter a congregation, discovering different ways congregations helped or hindered that movement. Since that research began we have held a number of conferences about what we learned; we have published numerous books and articles. What may not be obvious is the fact that all of this activity centered on the concept of the boundary. We saw that the newcomer, somehow, makes a decision to cross a boundary from not-in-the-congregation to in-the-congregation. We tried to find out what changed for them. How were they helped to learn the language of the new community? What barriers did the new community have in place that it might not even be aware of? We also recognized that the boundary-crosser generally sees things that natives do not see, so we asked the newcomer to help us map the congregation as they experienced it.

Any congregation can do what we did and learn a lot about itself from its newer members. The exercise would be more valuable than taking our findings and applying them second-hand.

In this time in which the paradigms are changing, the boundary between the congregation and the world outside has become more important than it has been for 1,600 years. Every lay person crosses that boundary twice a week. To be conscious of this is to be aware of one of the most exciting opportunities for research and for training that one could ever have. I believe that the concept of the boundary gives us a framework for developing some of the lay training we need for the church of the future.

The concept of boundary, however, is larger than this particular one, important as it is. Those who seek to build a church for the future will find it pays to pay attention to boundaries.

Steadiness

The discomfort of church structures with all the disruptions and changes of the present age has made church leaders anxious for new answers. That anxiety feeds what I call the "Tyranny of the New." There is a sense that only The New has value, so all our energy is used up inventing the new and marketing it. We rarely take time to install it well or to do the painstaking work of adapting it to the local situation. Rarely is time taken to see how what is new relates to what has been before.

When the new way is considered the only way, there is no continuity. Fads become the new Gospel, and in Paul's words, the church is "blown to and fro by every wind of doctrine." Particularly at times that require innovation, we need structures that hold steady, grounding The New, not allowing it to become erratic and impulsive.

We badly need church leaders, pastors, executives, and institutions that hold steady for the long pull. Without steadiness at the core, a steadiness that supports and studies the changes and innovations and then transmits the good to the next generation, the structures merely fibrillate anxiously and aimlessly.

I think this is a major concern for whatever paradigm we construct. Our fascination with The New and our faith in the rotation of leadership has eroded our ability to hold steady. The value we place on novelty is at war with our need to examine each novelty, discarding the useless and holding onto the valuable. In the past, steadiness frequently came from denominational identity, from institutional loyalties, and from trusted, steady leaders. None of those claim us as once they did.

Institutions have been an important source of steadiness in the past, but many of those we have known and trusted—like denominations— have lost some of their ability to hold us together. What new kinds of institutions do we need? Can the denominations themselves be reconfigured? Can seminaries rebuild themselves as the kind of institutions that can prepare leaders for a post-Christendom world? Can we find institutional frameworks through which to develop and deploy training and consulting skills to congregational leaders? Can the new institutions (e.g., The Alban Institute, the National Catholic Pastoral Center, the National Association of Evangelicals) find the resources to support congregations in new configurations? Will they be able to renew themselves?

What other institutions and leadership do we need for building the future church? Who will hold us steady on the future?

Accountability

The structures the churches developed in the first two-thirds of the twentieth century were fueled by a clear sense of mission to the far-off frontier. The financial and human resources needed for that frontier flowed into the churches because people who believed in mission saw the connection between what their churches did and what they understood mission to mean.

When that concept of mission began to shift in the 1930s and 1940s, the connection between local church and mission lost its clarity. The people in the denominational structures began to press for mission needs *they* perceived, but they did not make the connection clear to those in local churches. The message became something like: "You really cannot understand what mission really is; trust us and send us the resources." The people trusted and sent the resources. Floods of resources. But accountability suffered. Denominational program did reflect what denominational leaders deeply believed that mission was, but people in local churches were less and less convinced that it was what they understood as mission. Loyalty and trust held the system together for a long time. But loyalty eroded. Many committed Christian laypeople no longer trust that what their national denomination is doing is mission. And they do not trust what those people say.

I believe an analogy can be made to what has happened in Eastern Europe over the past fifty years. A cadre of leaders took power, assisted by the Soviet Union's armed forces. Those leaders had a clear sense of how a good society should be built, and they took the steps to do it. The citizens, by and large, accepted the painful consequences of a society and an economy that did not work very well in hope that their sacrifices would eventually produce that good society. Also, they did not have access to power or ways to change things.

At some point though, things stopped working. The people became unwilling to continue. They lost hope that things would get better. They stopped whatever support they had given to their governments out of previous loyalty or hope. At some point, in country after country in Eastern Europe, the establishment was challenged, and the socialist power structure blinked.

From the outside, the fall of the Berlin Wall was a dramatic surprise. In fact, the Wall had lost its strength a long time before, but nobody had pushed it. The will of the people had been withdrawn as they lost their trust in the system.

In Europe, people are finding answers very difficult to come by. Pushing over one ineffective system was deceptively easy. But what do you do *now*? Even though that system did not work, there still must be a system—an economy, a set of political parties, a way of making decisions and enforcing them.

I believe the societies of Eastern Europe foundered for the same reason that many of our denominational systems are in trouble. Leaders, committed to a real vision of what the mission of the state (church) is, shaped the life of the state (church) toward those ends. They lost the hearts and the trust of their people.

I believe we have been seeing evidence of similar disaffection for several decades in the denominations. The certainty of our leaders that they are leading toward mission has not been convincing to ordinary church members for some time.

For two thousand years Christians have sacrificially tried to get their best resources to the missionary frontier. Today that frontier has moved. Many members of congregations feel that their judicatories and denominations are using rhetoric about mission to secure support for activities that the members themselves do not understand to be mission. The nerve of trust has been cut.

Equally important in the long run, the judicatories and denominations have been slow to recognize how mission frontier has shifted. That may be because to do so is to raise serious questions about how and where the church spends its money. And until the churches begin seriously to make their structures accountable to the new missionary boundary, they will face continuing declines.

Those who work to build the future church will need to put energy into developing systems that promote clear accountability between those in congregations and those who assist them in mission. In The Alban Institute we have found the use of clear contracts between parties to be helpful in maintaining trust and accountability. We really believe a congregation ought to be able to fire us if we do not produce. Is the idea of a contract between a congregation and its judicatory out of the question? Are there better ways for accountability to be initiated once it has been damaged? Real work and imagination are needed at this point if congregations are going to get the kind of help they will need increasingly to face their mission frontier. Similarly, those in denominational structures may need to work through contractual systems to develop their ability to provide oversight and reestablish trust.

Building bridges and seeking allies

The process of building the new paradigm is already happening in countless communities. Five or six congregations (some members of whom would not be found dead or alive inside one of the others' churches during worship!) band together to address a community need—care for the homeless, support for local schools. Several denominations form a consortium to develop television ministries neither could handle alone. Lay people from different denominations and faiths band together to address drug problems.

In time, these connections may become as strong or stronger than the bonds of denominationalism. Most of them will be local or regional, not national. The national and international structures (councils of churches, etc.), which grew out of Christendom and linked denominational structures, may have the potential to make the kinds of connections needed, particularly on the local scene if they can move beyond fixation on survival.

Every Christian will need to seek allies in the mission into which he or she goes every week in the ambiguous world. Every congregation will need to build bridges to others to accomplish its mission.

Valuing failure

A church or congregation that moves ahead must be ready to value its failures, to expect many things not to work.

Many more things must be tried than can be expected to succeed. Building a climate that welcomes that kind of effort is not going to be easy. The church tends to honor only those who succeed and has been known to shoot its wounded.

If the church is going to meet the test of the next century, finding new vigor for its new mission, it simply must learn to honor and learn from the pioneers who do not make it over the Great Divide.

Faithfulness in the church has always been faithfulness in following the call. It has rarely meant winning.

Signs of the Future Church

The church of tomorrow is not yet visible. How it will configure itself we cannot know. What we can do, however, is note some signs of what it may be like—signs in the here and now that point to the character of what it may become in God's time. Each of these is a pointer toward something of what I believe the future church will be like:

- a Baptist congregation joins a Lutheran congregation and a Church of God congregation in establishing a watch program in neighborhoods where drugs are sold;

- a group of lawyers in a congregation issues an invitation to other lawyers in town to discuss forming a guild to start . talking about the role of law, faith, and community life;

- a group of Christians and nonChristians forms a local group to build homes for the homeless through Habitat for Humanity. Mission is fully present, but it begs questions of local religious structures;

- a seminary in a nearby town works with a group of Catholic congregations to develop a four-year night-school course for preparing parish lay workers. The lay workers take over major responsibilities in three parishes without resident priests;

- a group of skilled church professionals forms a partnership to provide consultative assistance to congregations and non-profit agencies facing difficult changes in their state. Soon they find a demand for their services in corporations and government agencies;

- a national denominational mission agency decides to focus on providing services instead of developing programs. It develops contracts with judicatory offices;

- people seeking depth and growth form a variety of twelve-step programs, many meeting in local churches. The spiritual power released in lives of individuals and families bypasses ordinary congregational programming. Local churches feel the power, but have a hard time knowing how to relate to the new life;

— an agency unrelated to any denomination builds a network of thousands of pastors, executives, and lay leaders committed to building better congregations and begins to broker knowledge among them;

— a seminary professor invents a way to give basic theological education to lay leaders and designs a way to deliver that education anywhere at nominal cost. Many congregations build their own lay seminaries as a result. Some of these become community seminaries of ministry, linking several congregations;

— pastors starting new congregations demand help from their denominations—and get it;

— a congregation, formed to be experimental, collapses after six years, and the members do a careful post-mortem for the denomination;

— a group of pastors with the unusual role of interim pastor decides to take responsibility for their specialty. They form a national support group independent of their denominations. They develop training and professional standards;

— executives and bishops from ten to twelve denominations take a full week each year to engage each other in learning how to carry out their jobs;

— a congregation joins one of another ethnic make-up in a tutoring program for elementary schools;

— a group of doctors, nurses, and medical technicians forms at a research hospital for weekly lunches and discussions of "the ministry of healing." No clergy are invited;

— a congregation facing the retirement of a pastor invites other congregations into a study of community needs of the next decade;

— a congregation just over a disastrous relationship with a pastor who sexually abused three members of the congregation hires a family therapist to help them grow and learn rather than avoid and hide;

— a congregation's board appoints one of its members to attend all city planning sessions;

— six congregations of different denominations set up a training program on new member ministries and coordinate their work for unchurched people of the community; and

— a congregation spawns four house-churches over a six-year period, and receives back members of two house-churches that came to an end after two and three years.

Each of us has probably seen signs like these. When they appear singly, they are not particularly dramatic. Each however, points beyond the Church of Christendom. Each is the tip of a possibility being born around us even now.

My hunch is that your congregation has some visible signs of the church that is being born. I would love to hear about them.

NOTES

1. Roy M. Oswald, *Crossing the Boundary* (Washington, DC: The Alban Institute, 1980).

2. Gary Harbaugh, William H. Behreus, Jill M. Hudson, and Roy M. Oswald, *Beyond the Boundary* (Washington, DC: The Alban Institute, 1986).

CHAPTER VI

Where in the World Is the Church Going?

A new church is being born around us. That is my thesis.

It is a church with deep roots in the past, shaped by the past. Its forms and roles and structures and institutions were formed to serve a great, but flawed, vision of its mission. On the whole, that past church—in spite of the faults and sinfulness intrinsic to human structures—served mission as well as it could. Looking back on it, there are many pages of history that we would change if we could, but I doubt that we would have done it better than they did.

The Christendom Paradigm is now rapidly fading. The great mission that undergirded its strength and fueled its growth is no longer clear. It leaves behind, however, powerful structures still shaped by it— structures of denominations and theology, hierarchy and priority, roles and relationships. Those structures still surround us, supporting us and frustrating us at the same time. The thought patterns of that church also continue to have power over us, for they shaped our consciousness as well as our institutions.

It is as if the magnetic North Pole moved from Greenland to Alaska, and our compasses keep flickering between the remembered pole and the new one. Our institutional compasses still point to Christendom while flickering toward the new orientation, the new pole. In such a world it is hard to keep one's bearings. The same is true of our own consciousness of our mission. It, too, flickers back and forth, making it hard to chart a straight course.

I have written this book because I believe we are called to engage with God in the process by which the new church comes into being. I believe the wisdom of lay leaders across the church, the faith of church people, the commitment of clergy, bishops, and executives, the skills of all leaders and members—*all* are invited and needed for the new to be discovered.

I do not expect clarity about the new church for several generations—I shall not see it, even though I work for it. That is true for most of us, I think. But perhaps there may be some of the young among us who will, like Moses, be led up to the high mountain from which at least to see the Promised Land.

What I have described as paradigms of the church and a changing paradigm of religious life is connected to equally radical changes of paradigms going on throughout the world. *Our* evolution is part of a cosmic evolution of nations and of consciousness, one that is reshaping evolution of East and West, of humanity and environment. What is happening to the church is part of the entire work of God, making all things new.

The evolution of the church is imbedded in and related to those great changes. God's call to a new world is the context of the call to the church.

The church's call is also very special within that larger framework. The evolution of the church holds up the pole of meaning within cosmic evolution. It holds up some key theses: that there is meaning and purpose in creation, that at the heart of creation is a loving, self-disclosing and self-giving Presence that broods over it all, breathing life into the whole of it. It holds those theses and witnesses to them against the antithesis of meaninglessness inherent in a mechanistic view of the story of creation.

It is that dialectic—meaning vs. meaninglessness—that is the driving power of history, not the minor dialectic of communism and capitalism that political economists have argued for the past century and a half.

It is no small thing to be part of an affirmation of meaning and purpose in the midst of chaos. The church hears the call to the new world as a call from the God who promises, not as the grinding of mechanical forces of necessity, moving inexorably to a determined denouement. The church hears the call as a call requiring response, commitment, and choice from a God who will not leave us comfortless.

But it is no comfort to speak of evolution. The word in recent generations has hidden a smug, simple faith in inevitable progress, a faith contradicted by scientific research as well as by the Christian faith. Modern science—from paleontology to physics—holds no brief for predictability, certainty, or progress. Those simple confidences, the legacy of Newton and Darwin, have not survived the the vast uncertainties of quantum physics and fossil studies of the Burgess Shale.

What we know now is that when change occurs, there is much that is unpredictable and uncertain. One cannot plan how to handle the next great California earthquake. One cannot know which species will survive the next cataclysms of nature. That mankind survived at all is not, science now tells us, the result of some innate superiority, but it is an extraordinary mystery. As Christians, we would say that it was the working out of grace, not of immutable forces.

As we take little comfort from an erroneous concept of progressive evolution, neither do we hear good news from our tradition. The story of the Hebrew people and of the New Testament people is a story of a troublesome pilgrimage. Rebellious, cowardly, treacherous, undependable, fractious, the biblical people have been a constant trial to their God. Their path is not a succession of great moments and great achievements. Their constant theme is the building of golden calves whenever things get difficult.

Why do we expect now to be any different? Why do we worry that "mainline" declines and "conservative" grows, and each envies the other? Two generations ago it was the reverse. Why do we wonder who will sit on the right hand of Jesus in his kingdom? Why do we make our theologies or political correctness the touchstone of our orthodoxy when Peter was told that all the animals in the great bedsheet let down from heaven were clean? Why are we surprised by the disappointing moral behavior of good Christian people—and, horrors, their pastors—when we read how the people in the Corinthian church lived?

Neither the concept of evolution nor the story of the faith gives us any confidence whatsoever that we shall make the right choices in moving from the Church of Christendom to the church God is calling to serve the world of the twenty-first century.

None whatsoever.

Those of us who share the biblical faith look at the uncertain future with normal human anxiety and fear, but also with a strange confidence that springs from knowing in Whose hands we are. We can look back at what our forebearers did and how they carried the faith. We can look at the institutions they built to house their life of faith. We can look at the shape of community that nurtured them. In what they did we can see flaws, but we can also see that there was a Presence with them in their wildernesses—in their false starts as well as in their successes. We can act now trusting in that same Presence. There is no other way for us.

A new church is being born. *It may not be the church we expect or want.* The church of the future may not include our favorite liturgy or hymn, our central theological principle, or even our denomination! God's promises always arrive with surprises in them. The form of the new world and new church is not in our hands.

What is in our hands is the chance to respond to God's call. To put our skills and our wills to the tasks of discerning the opportunity points, the places and times for change effort, and to add our gifts to God's church in this time of change. How God uses our gifts we cannot predict.

God is calling people across the face of this country and the world. God's call is to newness for the whole world, not just the church. Those of us who are called into the church have a special vocation to work for the renewal and refreshment of the church, not as an institution out of the past, but as a centering presence from which we may serve the new world that God is creating around us. We have been told that God is making all things new. God is calling us to participate in that new creation.

We have also been told that God's time is now.

APPENDIX

The Free Church Variation on Christendom

Many American denominations lived a significant variation on the paradigm I call "Christendom." All of the "Free" churches—those whose life is structured congregationally, including families such as Baptist and Congregational—have an order and a self-perception distinctly different from the model I have described in Chapter II.

In this appendix I want to speak to that difference and yet still argue for the strong influence of a "Christendom consciousness" within even those religious bodies that rejected an establishment role and a connectional polity (a system that makes congregations into federated or confederated families). The denominations that grew out of the European "establishments" and those that are "connectional" find the Christendom model more in their tradition.

In Ernst Troeltsch's distinction between "church" and "sect," Christendom speaks more to the experience of the continuum near "church."

First let me speak to the difference.

The appearance of groups of Christians who differed from the state religions was part of the ferment that gave rise to the Reformation of the sixteenth century. I want to focus on the experience in the churches of the British Isles for two reasons—it is the experience I am closest to and it is an experience that illustrates well the distinction I am driving at. Let us look at the situation as it developed in Anglican parishes *after* the Reformation, after the Civil Wars of the seventeenth century.

The English parish found within itself a different religious group, organized, worshipping, having fellowship in opposition to the local parish church. During the turmoil of the seventeenth century those religious differences had fought for domination, beginning with the assumption that the winner would replace the loser. The Pilgrims went to Holland and then to Massachusetts to get out of the oppressive religious climate of the English Parish Church and to set up a community in which their religious practice could be dominant. By the end of the wars a kind of exhausted, fairly distrustful truce had been established whereby the winners—the Anglican party in England, the Presbyterians in Scotland— accepted the fact that the losers existed and probably were around to stay.

Over several generations the majority community's perception of "the others" changed. From the seventeenth to the twentieth centuries it progressed from fear and suspicion, to grudging but careful co-existence, to a reluctant tolerance, to collaboration and cooperation. The government's attitude toward these nonestablishment religious groups changed from legal proscription to a kind of grudging second-class citizenship (the Act of Conformity is *important* because it granted the right of *existence* to the nonconformists). Today, the nonchurch of England citizen is not under legal restrictions because she or he is Methodist, Catholic, or Baptist.

But for *our* purposes, the issue is how the experience of being *in* a nonconformist congregation shaped relationship to society and to one's sense of mission. *(See Figure 5.)*

What has happened is that the nonconformist congregation inside the parish discovered a new boundary that separates it from the parish. It was a boundary of *religious practice* and *personal behavior*. Being part of the "chapel" rather than the parish, as the difference is still described today, stood for religious practice involving more attention to preaching and the Bible, a more enthusiastic worship and singing, and sometimes theological justification of the same. The lay person of these congregations saw this boundary as a requirement for more demanding personal piety and higher morality in business and community dealings.

Only the Quakers consistently witnessed that the boundary of mission was more dramatic, more all-inclusive. Only the Quakers from the beginning saw that the boundary of faith required them to witness against the laws of the state. For that reason they were the least tolerated of the nonconformist groups. The state couldn't care less how one prayed or sang if she or he still paid their taxes and served in the army. On those scores, Quakers—but generally not the other nonconformists— stopped preaching and started meddling.

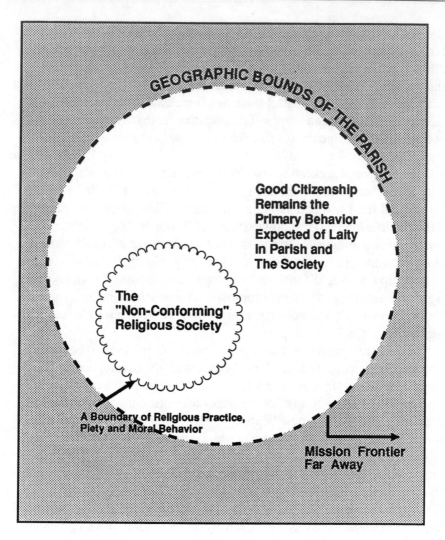

Figure 5

Over time the appearance of that *religious* demarcation line between congregation and parish became a critical turning point in the paradigm change this book is about.

Most of the American evangelical denominations drew important sustenance from that demarcation line. They discovered the importance of being different from the bland, inoffensive, subservient religion of the establishment.

Over time that ability to make *religious* differentiations from society led those people to understand the more radical differentiation of the people of faith from the political state.

Because people of congregations began to say, "we are different from the parish in how we study the Bible," they also were first to see and then say, "We are different, as Christians, from a government that permits slavery."

The boundary, once experienced in terms of religious practice, more and more became a boundary between one culture and another.

It is no surprise that Free Churches and evangelicals were the first to recognize social ills—slavery, the inhumanity of prisons and insane asylums, etc. What remains to be understood is how two extraordinary reversals took place—the first much discussed, the latter less so. The first reversal is how the powerful social activism of the evangelical and nonconforming denominations and groups reverted almost entirely to personal and religious values early in the twentieth century, becoming quite subservient to the Empire.

The less-discussed reversal is how the establishment churches, late in coming to an awareness of any boundary—religious or secular— between the Gospel and the Empire, developed a political infrastructure that became so intent on the boundary between the Gospel and the social and political realities that it lost touch with its religious constituency. There are books to be written about both, but not this book.

For our purpose it is important to note that the more a person or denomination has experienced the boundaries described in this appendix, the less compelling will their experience of Christendom have been.

Yet I argue that the climate of Christendom has affected the thought-patterns of the Free Churches nevertheless. The Christendom paradigm has been the dominant background thinking, the cultural myth. Even when personal experience rejects it, the culture has supported it.

There is another point. Within even the freest of the free denominations there seems to be a sort of gravitational pull toward what here I call "Christendom thinking." A Pentecostal friend from the Assemblies of God said to me, "Your description of Christendom sounds like a lot of stuff that keeps creeping up on us!" Troeltsch noted the tendency of sect over time to begin to adopt the behavior, structure, and stance of church.

This book describes the "church" experience. Those who have grown up in the churches of the great informal American establishment will identify most with the argument. Those who grew up in another experience of congregation will find some elements over- or under-emphasized, but I believe they will find important implications for their religious systems.

In the final analysis, the issue is one of mission. How do we as Christians—whether mainline or sideline, liberal or conservative, connectional or free—find a community that forms and sustains us in an authentic faith and move out bearing that faith into the structures of our ambiguous society? How do we pass those forms of community on to the next generation?

$\mathcal{W}$elcome to the work of Alban Institute...

**the leading publisher and congregational
resource organization for clergy and laity today.**

Your purchase of this book means you have an interest in the kinds of information, research, consulting, networking opportunities and educational seminars that Alban Institute produces and provides. Founded in 1974, we are a non-denominational, non-profit membership organization dedicated to providing practical and useful support to religious congregations and those who participate in and lead them.

Alban is acknowledged as a pioneer in learning and teaching on *Conflict Management *Faith and Money *Congregational Growth and Change *Leadership Development *Mission and Planning *Clergy Recruitment and Training *Clergy Support, Self-Care and Transition *Spirituality and Faith Development *Congregational Security.

Our membership is comprised of over 8,000 clergy, lay leaders, congregations and institutions who benefit from:

- ❖ 15% discount on hundreds of Alban books
- ❖ $50 per-course tuition discount on education seminars
- ❖ Subscription to *Congregations*, the Alban journal (a $30 value)
- ❖ Access to Alban research and (soon) the "Members-Only" archival section of our web site www.alban.org

For more information on Alban membership, books, consulting, and leadership enrichment seminars, visit our Web Site: **www.alban.org** or call **1-800-486-1318, ext.243.**

The Alban Institute
Bethesda, MD